The World According To

# PETER DRUCKER

JACK BEATTY

THE FREE PRESS

*New York   London   Toronto   Sydney   Singapore*

*f*P

THE FREE PRESS
A Division of Simon & Schuster Inc.
1230 Avenue of the Americas
New York, NY 10020

THE FREE PRESS and colophon are trademarks
of Simon & Schuster Inc.

Designed by Carla Bolte

Manufactured in the United States of America

10  9  8  7  6  5  4  3  2  1

Library of Congress Cataloging-in-Publication Data

Beatty, Jack.
   The world according to Peter Drucker / Jack Beatty.
      p.     cm.
   Includes index.
   ISBN 0–684–83801–X
   1. Management—History.   2. Drucker, Peter Ferdinand, 1909–       .
I. Drucker, Peter Ferdinand, 1909–       .   II. Title.
HD30.5.B4   1998
658.4'0092—dc21                                      97–36988
[B]                                                  CIP

To Lois, with love

Three of the Eleven Categories of Products:

1. Today's breadwinners

2. Tomorrow's breadwinners

3. Yesterday's breadwinners

—*Managing for Results* (1964)

# Contents

# Acknowledgments

M<small>Y</small> <small>PRIMARY</small> debt of gratitude is to Peter Drucker for agreeing to sit for this intellectual portrait, for answering my rookie questions with patient tact, and for fact-checking the manuscript. It says a great deal about Mr. Drucker's character that the one change in substance he lobbied for had to do with the accuracy of economic statistics not with my judgments of his work, however critical. Peter and Doris Drucker took time out of their busy lives—Doris is an entrepreneur launching a new product as well as the author of an elegant witty memoir, "Invent Radium or I'll Pull Your Hair"—to share their hospitality with me, for which I am very grateful.

My second debt is to William Whitworth, the editor in chief of the *Atlantic Monthly,* where I work. This book could not have been written without his help. My thanks also to my colleagues Cullen Murphy, Martha Spaulding, Barbara Wallraff, Corby Kummer, and Michael Curtis for shouldering many of my *Atlantic* burdens.

To Bob Buford, Don and Carol Mitchell, Bill Johnston, Rand Castile, Charles Ellis, Frances Hesselbein, Vincent Barabba, Michael Mufson, and Charles Magraw—my warmest thanks. Matthew Dalleck took time away from his forthcoming Free Press book on the origins of modern political campaigning to help me research this book—thanks, Matt. Chris Berdick, an *Atlantic* intern, helped too—thanks, Chris.

Special thanks to my agent, Rafe Sagalyn, whose belief in this book launched it; to my editor at The Free Press, Bruce Nichols, whose professional judgment made it possible; and to Robert Harrington, for his editorial supervision.

My sister, Joan R. Bond, died suddenly while I was at work on the book: a dedicated and gifted teacher, a witty and enlivening presence, a loving mother and grandmother, Joan is missed painfully by all who loved her.

My son, Aaron, bore charitably with his preoccupied father, who loves him. I dedicate this book to my wife, Lois, who improved every page.

Jack Beatty
August 21, 1997

The World According To

# PETER
# DRUCKER

# Prologue

THE PRESIDENT knew the man needed no introduction, so, without a word of identification, he simply told the employees of the Department of Health, Education, and Welfare assembled to hear his speech: "Peter Drucker says that modern government can do only two things well: wage war and inflate the currency. It's the aim of my administration to prove Mr. Drucker wrong." If Richard Nixon thought he did not have to identify Peter Drucker thirty years ago, must I do it now? Drucker's fame is planetary. (The test of planetary is to have one of your novels be a best seller in Brazil.) According to a recent book on management gurus, Peter Drucker is "one of the few thinkers in any discipline who can claim to have changed the world: he is the inventor of privatization, the apostle of a new class of knowledge workers, the champion of management as a serious discipline." Drucker has been called everything from "the father of management" to "the man who changed the face of industrial America" to "the one great thinker management theory has produced." On inspection these and other encomia about him turn out to be within caviling distance of being true. This book attempts to show why.

# 1

# A Singular Education

PETER DRUCKER'S earliest memory captures one of the worst moments of the twentieth century. He was in the children's bathroom, just above his father's study, and through the heating register he could hear three voices. One belonged to his father, the senior civil servant in the Ministry of Economics of the Austro-Hungarian government; the second to his uncle, one of Vienna's leading jurists; the third to Thomas Masaryk, the future president of Czechoslovakia. Not yet five, Peter couldn't be sure who, but one of them clearly said, "This is the end not just of Austria, but of civilization." It was August 1914. The Great War had just begun.[1]

Earlier that summer the Druckers—his father, Adolph, his mother, Caroline, and his younger brother, Gerhart—taking a long-planned vacation on the Adriatic seashore, had barely settled on the beach when news came of the Archduke Ferdinand's assassination in Sarejevo. The assassin was a terrorist operating from (though not, as it turned out, *for*), the independent country of Serbia, which bordered Bosnia, a province of Austria-Hungary since 1908. Serbia was protected by Russia, which was tied by treaty to France as France was to Britain and as Austria-Hungary was to Germany. The war party in Vienna seized on the assassination, for which they held Serbia responsible, as a pretext for crushing Serbia, a long-time imperial goal. The twisting fuse of alliances, however, worked against localization of the conflict to the Balkans. Any Austrian retaliation against Serbia risked general European war.[2]

A colleague sent Adolph Drucker a telegram urging him to return to Vienna immediately to stop the rush toward war. (So Adolph later told his son, who remembered only his mother's funny bathing suit from that shrouded holiday.) The "known liberals and pacifists" in the ranks of the senior civil servants, Adolph said, had taken it upon themselves "to lobby our ministers, buttonhole politicians, try to get to the old emperor through the wall of equally old courtiers," to head off the catastrophe. They failed: by declaring war on Serbia and shelling the Serbian capital, Belgrade, Austria-Hungary struck the fateful match.[3]

The war haunted Peter Drucker's childhood, though, as we will see, it also expedited his career as a writer. He and his friends taught themselves to read "by scanning the casualty lists and the obituaries with the big black borders, looking for names we knew, names of people we loved and missed." To them war was a permanent condition of the world. "None of us could imagine that the war would ever end," Drucker recalls. "Indeed every boy my age *knew* that 'When I grow up' meant 'When I get drafted and sent to the front.'"[4]

A few years later, when Drucker was a senior in high school, his class was assigned to review the first crop of books to appear on the war. "When we then discussed these . . . in class, one of my fellow students said, 'Every one of these books says that the Great War was a war of total military incompetence. Why was it?' Our teacher did not hesitate a second but shot right back, 'Because not enough generals were killed; they stayed way behind the lines and let others do the fighting and dying.'" In this the members of Drucker's generation shared something in common with the generals. They were spared. Drucker is conscious of his luck in being too young to be used as cannon fodder by those murderously incompetent generals. "Those of us who have been spared the horrors in which our age specializes," he wrote in *Landmarks of Tomorrow* (1959), "who have never suffered total war, slave-labor camp or police terror, not only owe thanks; we owe charity and compassion."[5]

If the war brought fear, the peace brought hunger. The winter of 1919–1920 was grim. "Like practically every child in Vienna," Drucker writes in his sparkling autobiography, *Adventures of a Bystander* (1979), "I was saved by Herbert Hoover whose feeding organization provided school lunches. They left me with a lasting aversion to porridge and cocoa—but definitely saved my life and that of millions of children throughout Continental Europe." An "organization" did all that good. One sees the biographical roots of Drucker's concept of organization as an instrument of human creativity.

The Hoover mission, noteworthily, was also a triumph of management, though the word was unknown in its current sense then. As we will see, Peter Drucker would explore one of the largest organizations in the world, General Motors, in his career-long inquiry into history's first "society of organizations" and the role of management in that society. More, in the "manager" he would discover an unacknowledged author of modernity, a culture hero to rival the totemic figure of the artist.

THE DRUCKERS lived in suburban Vienna in a modish house built for them by a prominent Viennese architect. Through the mansard window of his first grown-up room under the eaves, Peter could see, past the local vineyards, the hills of the Vienna Woods. The Druckers were "good class" professional people. Adolph was an economist and lawyer; Caroline had studied medicine—quite rare for a woman in the Austria of those days, and they shared their professional interests with their children. "My father had a dinner party every

Monday," Drucker says. "There were often economists, ranking civil servants, even a major international lawyer." Later in the week, his mother held a medical dinner. There were musical dinners (his grandmother was a soloist with the Vienna Philharmonic under the baton of Gustav Mahler) and literary dinners. Improbably, there were even mathematics dinners: "My father and mother were very interested in mathematics and philosophy." Imagine trying to wring conviviality out of calculus.[6]

At one dinner he heard a medical eminence attack Freud, then the most famous man in Vienna, for his unfeeling detachment from his suffering patients—a breach of the physician's "sacred duty" to be a compassionate healer. At another a "moderately pro-Freudian" psychologist and young Oskar Morgenstern, destined for Princeton, where he became "the foremost authority on statistical theory," debated a study of the therapeutic efficacy of psychoanalysis, the psychologist saying it showed promising results, Morgenstern entering a statistical demur: "Not so, if you go by the figures, then there are either no emotional illnesses at all or the trust of the patient in any method makes the patient feel better, regardless of method." To which another dinner guest, a surgeon (inevitably), responded, "In either case there is as yet no valid Freudian psychotherapy which a physician can recommend or use in good conscience." Readers of Drucker, curious about his penchant for scientific and, especially, medical metaphors, need look no further than those evenings.[7]

His literary allusions—Jane Austen nimbly surfacing in a discussion of the evolution of military technology; or Henry James adding a dollop of unlikely relevance on the topic of the industrial working class—spring from a similar social-cultural source. Besides the standard elevated fare he was fed at home, young Peter was also a habitué of a salon presided over by one of the Druckers' closest friends. There he heard the American journalist, Dorothy Thompson, discuss current affairs; saw Count Helmuth Moltke, who would be "at the center of the resistance to Hitler," display "the magnetism of the born leader"; and listened, bored, as Thomas Mann read his short novel *Disorder and Early Sorrow.* Culture was also heavily laid on every Christmas and New Years, when a leading Viennese actress, Maria Mueller, dined with the Druckers and then recited from memory scenes from Greek tragedy, Goethe, Schiller, and, in English, from Shakespeare: "*King Lear, The Tempest* and—her favorite as well as mine—*Cymbeline.*"

Even among his playmates Drucker encountered intellectual distinction. "One day we played 'What are you going to be when you grow up?' And we were saying policeman or fireman—except for Gustav, who said, 'I am going to be Professor of Islamic Studies at the University.' It scared me spitless, because somehow I knew that Gustav would carry it out." Gustav went on to hold a chair in Islamic Studies at the University of Chicago.[8]

If Drucker had never spent a day in school, he'd still be superbly well educated by ear, from the high multilingual talk flowing over him. Besides heaps of esoteric knowledge, these occasions lent him the style of casual sophistication that distinguishes his writing. Learning is his mind's pleasure, a gift to share with his readers, not an invitation to pomposity. The Druckers raised an intellectual, not an academic.

For sixty years Drucker has taken on a new subject every three or four years and read up on it to the capacious limits of his curiosity. One year it might be Japanese art, which he taught on the side for six years at Pomona College; another year it could be sixteenth-century finance; yet another the history of technology or of work—or of American statesmen or of British rule in India. He recommends intellectual omnivorousness as a form of self-renewal. Certainly it has worked for him. A recent issue of *Forbes,* with Drucker's picture on the cover, bore the nearly plausible title "Still the YOUNGEST MIND." Drucker's reading also pays off on the page. Few other "management gurus" can garnish a paragraph with bits like this: "It is no accident that the word 'risk' itself in the original Arabic meant 'earning one's daily bread.'" (Had you forgotten that?) "Only in Drucker," the *Economist* notes, "would you learn that the first management conference was organized in 1882, by the German Post Office—and that nobody showed up." Even more characteristic is Drucker's use of historical analogies, often felicitous. Thus in discussing ways to deter polluters of the "Transnational Ecology," he notes that, "The nineteenth century cured two of mankind's oldest scourges, the slave trade and piracy on the high seas, by transnational action." As the 19th century did with piracy, so the twenty-first can do with pollution. Drucker's books teach; above everything, he is a teacher.[9]

He had become "incurably infected" with "the teaching bug" in fourth grade, when he became the apt pupil of "Miss Elsa" and "Miss Sophy," two sisters who taught in a progressive private school to which his parents transferred him from a state school to redeem his handwriting. Miss Sophy, the warmer of the two, was an educational innovator. She taught the boys to cook and sew and the girls to hammer and saw, a then "revolutionary doctrine" that was also the rule at home, where Caroline Drucker tackled the repairs, including plumbing and reshingling. If Miss Elsa offered terse encouragement ("Better than last week"), Miss Sophy smiled—"the only praise she ever gave, but one that was pure bliss to the beholder."[10]

Dressed in forbidding black bombazine that lent her the aspect of a "big beetle," with pince-nez and high-button shoes, Miss Elsa could be severe. Yet, ". . . we worshipped her," Drucker says. "When fifty years later, the Women's Libbers announced that the Lord is really a woman, I was not a bit surprised."[11]

Miss Elsa devised a way to make Peter responsible for his own learning. She gave him a notebook and required him to record what he expected to learn at the beginning of each week and then to check his expectations against the results at the end of the week. (Miss Elsa, it appears, invented "Managing by Objectives," Drucker's signature management concept.) By fourth grade Peter was showing promise as a writer. "I knew fairly early in life," he says, "that writing was one thing I was likely to do well—perhaps the only thing." Recognizing and reinforcing his strength, Miss Elsa had him write two compositions every week, one on a subject of her choosing, the other on one of his. By thus working on what he did well, she first modeled the credo Drucker has imparted to executives for over fifty years: focus on what people *can* do, not on what they *can't* do. Schools concentrate more on problems than on strengths. As a result "people don't know what they do well because they are not encouraged to think that way. That's probably my greatest strength as both a teacher and consultant—I immediately look for that." He generalizes to others the method of his own learning. "I realized that I, at least, do not learn from mistakes. I have to learn from successes."[12]

Drucker was the first to name the "knowledge worker," the first to chart the emerging "knowledge society." Yet he warns of a new "mandarinate" of the credentialed. "By asking the schoolmaster to pick management," he wrote in *The New Society* in 1950, when this trend was barely visible, "the enterprise will deny itself the very men it needs most: the entreprenuer, the innovator, the risk-taker." Forty years later, in *The New Realities,* he used history to make the same, and by then commonplace, point: "Neither Gottlieb Daimler nor Henry Ford would have much chance to get to the top without an engineering degree or an MBA. No reputable financial firm would be likely today to hire the 'college dropout' J. P. Morgan."

Not how long or where you went to school, but how you *perform* is the only fair test of an employee. Yet, increasingly, you won't get to be an employee unless your ticket gets punched (and punched again) in the costly groves of academe. American business has long been the most democratic proscenium in American life. Ordinary people got the chance to do extraordinary things. To succeed in business you didn't have to go to Harvard. Indeed, that could hurt you. As recently as the mid-1950s Drucker was told of a Sears' executive, "He got promoted at Sears even though he went to Harvard Law School." But this egalitarian tradition of American business is being eaten away by the growth of a "mandarin meritocracy," a trend worrying to Drucker.[13]

THOUGH PETER had failed to improve his handwriting, he was otherwise sufficiently advanced that Miss Elsa urged the Druckers to have him skip fifth grade and go directly from fourth grade to the state-run Latin school, the Gymnasium. Gymnasium proved challenging only to Peter's memory. "I spent eight years . . . on Latin irregular verbs. . . . There was hardly a hint from any of the teachers that Horace or Tacitus might be read except to find their grammatical mistakes." Drucker weathered the tedium "by reading history and the world's great literature under the desk."[14]

At least one teacher in these years, however, left a lasting mark. When he was thirteen an "inspiring teacher of religion" gave him an invaluable life-lesson by asking each student what he wanted to be remembered for. Of course they were too young to answer. "So he chuckled and said, 'I didn't expect you to be able to answer it. But if you still can't answer it by the time you're fifty, you will have wasted your life.'" Drucker has tried to live by that existential imperative ever since. "I am always asking that question . . . It is a question that induces you to renew yourself—because it pushes you to see yourself as a different person—the person you can *become*."[15]

DRUCKER HAD wanted to leave Vienna for years. As soon as he could, after finishing Gymnasium, he got out. Once capital of a vast and variegated empire of 50 million that stretched from the Alps to the borders of Russia, postwar Vienna had become, A. J. P. Taylor writes, "the inflated capital of a small Alpine country" of 6.5 million, paying a huge price for losing the war its imperial rulers had started. The city lived in the past, in a saccharine fog of nostalgia for "prewar," when, Taylor notes, "Vienna was a German-speaking Paris with even larger cafes and even gayer life." "All they talked about was life before 1914," Drucker says. "I was surrounded by extinct volcanoes . . ." Much to his father's distress, instead of going straight to the university and then, perhaps, to medical school, as his brother was expected to do, Peter took an apprentice's job in Hamburg. "I had sat [in school] long enough. I would be an adult among other adults—I had never liked being young, and detested the company of delayed adolescents as I thought most college students to be. I would earn a living and be financially independent." He was seventeen.[16]

In Hamburg he worked as clerk-trainee for an export firm that sold hardware to India. His hours were from 7:30 A.M. to 4:00 P.M. on weekdays and until noon on Saturdays, which gave him and two other trainees the balance of the weekend to hike in the country around Hamburg. "To appease my father," he says, "but without any serious intention, I enrolled at Hamburg University in the Law faculty." He thought of himself as a part-time student. "Full-time law students did not spend four years working hard and studying the law. They spent four years in an agreeable haze compounded of two parts beer and one part sex." He figured he "could get quite enough of both" without going full-time. But there was a Kafkaesque complication. The University did not hold evening classes; and he worked during the day— so how could he be any sort of student? It was enough, in those days of academic vagabondage, to enroll in a course and take an exam at the end of the term to get credit. "During my entire year and a half in Hamburg, I therefore did not attend a single class at the university."[17]

Instead he spent five weekday evenings reading in the Hamburg

City Library. "For fifteen months, I read, and read, and read in German and English and French." Once a week he went to the Hamburg Opera and there he made a life-changing discovery. After watching a performance of *Falstaff,* Verdi's last opera, he was astonished and moved to find that Verdi had written this high-spirited work when he was eighty. Asked why he had taken up such a challenging opera at his age, Verdi had said, "All my life as a musician I have striven for perfection. It has always eluded me. I surely have an obligation to make one more try." Those words made "an indelible impression" on Drucker. Although he was only eighteen, he pledged to go at his life's work in Verdi's spirit. He further resolved "that if I ever reached an advanced age, I would not give up, but would keep on." Writing four books since *he* reached eighty, he has kept to Verdi's course. "Whenever people ask me which of my books I consider the best, I smile and say, 'The next.' "[18]

He stayed just over a year in Hamburg, where he launched his career as a writer with two scholarly papers, both in the field of economics—the stuff of table talk at the Druckers. One was on the Panama Canal's role in world trade; the other, an econometric analysis of the New York stock market. Published in the September 1929 issue of a prestigious economic journal, it confidently predicted that the market could only go up. Just weeks later, in October, the market crashed. Drucker says this was the last financial prediction he ever made. "Fortunately, there is no copy of the journal left."[19]

Luckily, his stock market paper had not yet been published when the Frankfurt branch of a Wall Street firm hired him as a trainee security analyst. He lasted there until the Great Crash put the firm out of business. He had learned a valuable lesson about the impenetrable caprice of markets.

TRANSFERRING HIS law school courses to Frankfurt University, Drucker also enrolled in a statistics course "because I was head over heels in love with the beautiful wife of my boss—and she was a statistics student at the University." Post Crash, he accepted an offer to be the financial writer on Frankfurt's largest daily newspaper, the *Frankfurter General Anzeiger*. Soon, he was promoted to senior editor. He was to handle all foreign and all economic news, to write six to eight editorials a week, and, that editor being ill, to run the women's pages. A senior editor on a major newspaper at twenty? The war had cut down the generation before Drucker's. The German and Austrian thirty-five-year-olds who should have been the senior writers and editors were dead. "This situation was not too different," Drucker notes, spanning continents and wars, "from what I found in Japan when I first went there ten years after the end of the Pacific War, in the mid- and late fifties."[20]

His new boss, Erich Dombrowski, one of the leading liberal editors in Germany, was Drucker's third great teacher. A Prussian for punctuality, he chastised Drucker on his first day on the job for showing up at 6:10 A.M. That the streetcar did not start running in time was not an acceptable excuse. Walk! "We began at 6 in the morning and finished by a quarter past 2 in the afternoon, when the last edition went to press," Drucker says. "So I began to force myself to study afternoons and evenings: international relations and international law; the history of social and legal institutions; finance; and so on." Since, "A journalist has to write about many subjects," he was steeping himself in as many as he could.

Twice yearly Dombrowski convened a come-to-Jesus meeting beginning on Saturday afternoon and lasting all day Sunday to review the work of his small staff over the preceding six months. What had they done well? What had they tried to do well? What had they not tried hard enough to do? He would then launch into a "scathing critique" of what they had done badly. Looking ahead to the next six months, each staffer would then say what he should focus on, what he should improve, and what he should learn—Miss Elsa's very method. Drucker

eventually adopted it himself; he spends two weeks every summer cat-
echizing his year's work à la Dombrowski. "Keeping score on yourself"
in this way is the "best of the nuts and bolts of self development. . . .
Keeping score helps me to focus my efforts in areas where I have an
impact and to slough off projects where nothing is happening." Demanding as Dombrowski was, he listened to Peter and gave him responsibility, a huge word in the Drucker lexicon.[21]

Frankfurt University proved as much an academic snooze as Hamburg. Still, Drucker sampled at least one course that greatly influenced
him. Indeed, it gave him a model for the *discipline* of management. Of
all things it was a course on admiralty law. This would seem a narrow
subject, but the teacher presented admiralty law as a microcosm of
Western history, society, technology, legal thought, and economy.
Drucker regards this as "the most general education I ever had. . . ."
Fifteen years later, he used the course as template for teaching management. Like admiralty law, management can seem a narrow specialty.
Drucker, however, has taught it as "an integrating discipline of human
values and conduct, of social order and intellectual inquiry," one that
"feeds off economics, psychology, mathematics, political theory, history, and philosophy. In short, management is a *liberal art*. . . ."[22]

Because he was not a German citizen, he was not eligible to take
the state examination for a law doctorate. So, by cramming and by a fa-
cility in taking tests, he received a fairly pointless doctorate in public
law and international relations. His topic: the status of "almost governments"—rebellions, governments in exile, colonies about to be independent—under international law. "The one thing I got out of being a
law student," he says, "was that I met Doris—not in a lecture I attended (I didn't attend any) but in one I taught to substitute for the international law professor who was sick." Doris Schmitz, a young
German woman from Mainz, would become Drucker's wife of sixty
years.[23]

\*    \*    \*

IT WAS the early 1930s now. Black-shirted Nazi thugs were on the streets. "All around me society, economy, and government—indeed civilization—were collapsing." To answer the sickness of the times, Drucker was drawn to three German thinkers who had tried to create order amidst the upheavals of their own times. "I began to write a book that would make it impossible for the Nazis to have anything to do with me." It would be an intellectual biography of Wilhelm von Humbolt (1767–1835), among other distinctions founder of the University of Berlin; Joseph von Radowitz (1797–1853), the godfather of Europe's Catholic political parties; and Friedrich Julius Stahl (1802–1861), a legal philosopher, an accomplished parliamentarian—and a Jew.[24]

In the event, Drucker finished only the essay on Stahl, "which in the name of conservatism and patriotism put him forth as the exemplar and preceptor for the turbulence of the 1930s." As Drucker had anticipated, this was intolerable to the Nazis. Published in April 1933, two months after Hitler took power, the Stahl pamphlet was promptly banned and, indeed, burned. Knowing that he would soon be "kicked out or jailed," Drucker decided to leave Germany. Still, he "dawdled and hung on."[25]

Through the years of Hitler's rise to power, Drucker had begun to take the complex measure of fascism. In his first book, *The End of Economic Man: The Origins of Totalitarianism,* published in 1939, he plumbed its irrationalism and nihilism. "It is antiliberal, but also anticonservative; antireligious and antiatheist; anticapitalist and antisocialist; antiwar and antipacifist; against big business, but also against small artisans and shopkeepers. . . ." He witnessed a "wildly cheering" rally of peasants at which a Nazi logician gave a vivid demonstration of "the abracadabra of fascism" with this burst of irrationality: "We don't want lower bread prices, we don't want higher bread prices, we don't want

unchanged bread prices—we want National-Socialist bread prices."
He also glimpsed the naked cynicism of the Nazi leaders, attending a
rally where Goebbels, after telling a "particularly choice lie" that sent
his audience into raptures, added, "Of course, you understand all this
is just propaganda," which elicited a frenzy of cheers.[26]

The spur that finally drove him out of Germany was a faculty
meeting at the university led by its newly appointed "Nazi commissar."
Drucker went to the meeting hopeful that the famously liberal faculty
of Germany's most "self-confidently liberal" university would defend
intellectual freedom. The Nazi began by announcing that Jewish faculty members would be dismissed forthwith. Then he harangued the
faculty in foul language—"It was nothing but 'shit' and 'fuck' and
'screw yourself'." When he subsided all eyes turned to the Nobel-
quality biochemist, a famous liberal. He would put the Nazi goon in
his place. "The great liberal got up, cleared his throat, and said: 'Very
interesting, Mr. Commissar, and in some respects very illuminating.
But one point I didn't get too clearly. Will there be more money for research in physiology?'"

"Although a few of the non-Jewish faculty left in solidarity with
their Jewish colleagues, most did not. I went out sick unto death—and
I knew I would leave Germany within forty-eight hours."[27]

WITHOUT KNOWING a single person there, Drucker moved
to London, taking a job as a securities analyst for an insurance company. One day, while going up on the long escalator in the Piccadilly
Circus tube station, he passed Doris Schmitz coming down. They
waved madly to each other, and when Peter reached the top he got on
the down escalator, while Doris, on reaching the bottom, got on the
up. After passing each other again, they sorted things out. Doris was
taking courses at the London School of Economics, and in London she
and Peter began their courtship.[28]

The insurance job ended just before Christmas 1933, and it was a discouraged young man who returned to Vienna to spend the holidays with his parents. A taste of Vienna, however, steeled his will to return to job-scarce (there was a depression on) London to make a new start on his career—whatever that was to be. But Doris was much the stronger reason to return. "With every day away from her it became more apparent to me that I wanted to be with her and had to be where she was."[29]

His father asked him to take back a cuckoo clock for an "old friend" in London. The clock delivered, Drucker had lunch with this friend, who, on hearing of his work history, offered him a job as economist, asset manager, and general secretary for a small merchant bank. He stayed at the firm for almost four years, until the job crossed the low threshold of his boredom, and he left Europe for America.[30]

During this English interlude, Drucker discovered that he was not an economist. Every week he took the train down to Cambridge University to attend John Maynard Keynes' seminar. While literally sitting at the great man's feet he "suddenly realized that Keynes and all the brilliant economics students in the room were interested in the behavior of commodities while I was interested in the behavior of people." His interest in people would lead him to the study of management, which, seeming to be about commodities, is for Drucker all about people. It would lead as well to his career as a management consultant. "This is a person business," he'd say about consulting. "We are not greengrocers selling commodities." As for economics, "There is only one point on which the economists and I are in agreement: I am NOT an economist." And as for Keynesian economics, notably its advice to governments to spend their way out of depressions, "It was like a doctor telling you that you have inoperable liver cancer, but it will be cured if you go to bed with a beautiful seventeen-year-old."[31]

As early as 1935, Drucker had begun publishing in American periodicals ranging from the *Virginia Quarterly Review* to the *Saturday Evening Post*. London had palled for him. People there, as in Vienna, obsessively repaired to "prewar" even as a new war loomed inexorably. In his bones Drucker wanted to be quit of the past and, in a striking phrase he applies in one of his books to the Founding Fathers, to "solve the future." America, future-facing, drew him. He would launch his career here as a political scientist, but his interest in the behavior of people would not find repletion in the abstractions of political theory, and he would soon turn to the study of organizations, beginning with an American social innovation, the large corporation. In January 1937 he and Doris were married. Mere days later they left for America, Peter representing several large British papers, including the then *Financial News* and now *Financial Times*. He did not, however, come to the US as a correspondent. Instead, "I came as a writer."[32]

TO COME is a chapter on Drucker's mastery of modern English prose; then begins the long march through his books. That will proceed chronologically, though we will also seek to bring his whole work to bear on any part of it.

# 2

# "I Write"

"Since i was twenty," Drucker wrote at eighty-two, "writing has been the foundation of everything I have been doing, such as teaching and consulting." Over his sixty-year career Drucker has published twenty-nine books, an average of one book every two years. His oeuvre falls into three categories: books of social and political analysis like *The Future of Industrial Man* (1942) and *The Age of Discontinuity* (1969), books on management like *The Practice of Management* (1954), and *Management: Tasks, Responsibilities, Practices* (1974), and books of practical advice to managers like *Managing for Results* (1964) and *The Effective Executive* (1966). In addition, he regularly collects his essays in books like *The Frontiers of Management* (1986) and *The Ecological Vision* (1993). Asked how many copies his books have sold altogether, with a nonchalance about magnitudes to make all writers weep, Drucker says, "Five or six million."[1]

But books are only the half of it. Drucker has for years poured forth streams of articles. From 1975 to 1995, he wrote a widely-quoted monthly column for the editorial page of the *Wall Street Journal*. Over these same years—"the period of my greatest productivity," he calls it—he wrote twenty-two long pieces of 3500 to 6500 words each: eight for the *Harvard Business Review*, three for *The Public Interest*, three for *The Atlantic Monthly*, two for *Foreign Affairs*, two for *The Economist*, and one each for *New Perspectives, Inc., Forbes,* and *Esquire.* He collected his best essays over fifty years in *The Ecological Vision.* He bundled twenty years' worth of essays into three of what he calls "planned" essay volumes for which he selects the main topics before he writes the first piece. And he wrote two novels. He also managed to write three management books and four books on "Society, Economics, and Politics," including his most recent book, *Drucker on Asia,* which was originally written for the Japanese market and which came out in English in 1997 and is now being translated into Korean, Portuguese, German, French, Spanish, and Thai.

He writes these hundreds of thousands of words in a small, airy study in his comfortable ranch-style house on an ordinary suburban street in Claremont, California. He uses an electronic typewriter. "I don't use the word processor because it makes me too verbose," he says. Asked what he does, he answers, in all truth, "I write."

And he lectures—now mostly via satellite; and consults. In one four-month period of 1997, he held fourteen days of lectures and seminars. Most of these were all-day affairs, and, in line with his practice of fifty years, half were paid, half *pro bono.* He also had five full-day consulting engagements, three paid, two *pro bono.* Two were with large multinational manufacturing companies; two with nonprofits (*pro bono*), one American, one Argentinian. He also made, as he does yearly, a series of five 35-minute educational videos, mostly sold in Europe, Latin America, and East Asia. He also gave five three-hour interviews—three to US publications (one of which, *Forbes,* made the interview its cover piece), one each to a Brazilian and a French magazine.

He also teaches. He has two big ("I like them big") classes, one in the Claremont Graduate School's Executive Management Program, one in its MBA program—largely with foreign students with years of work experience and responsible jobs in their own countries. "I much prefer teaching students with management experience," he says. Many years ago he turned down an invitation to teach at the Harvard Business School because it was then full of students fresh from college. "Students without a good deal of experience don't learn anything from me," he says, "because I don't learn anything from them."[2]

Given his marathon prolificacy Drucker's answer to a question from an interviewer for *Inc.* comes as no surprise:

*Q:* What do you do with your leisure time?

*A:* What leisure time? . . .[3]

"Know Thy Time," Drucker counsels executives. He takes his own advice. Write him asking if he will speak to your group or review a book for your magazine (as I did); and Drucker, who has no secretary, will send you a postcard with this efficient legend printed on the back:

**Mr. Peter F. Drucker**

greatly appreciates your kind interest, but is unable to:

contribute articles or forewords; comment on manuscripts or

books; take part in panels or symposia; join committees or

boards of any kind; answer questionnaires; give

interviews; and appear on radio and television.

Receiving this card after requesting an interview, John Tarrant reports in his *Drucker: The Man Who Invented Corporate Society* (1976), one journalist sent it back with an acerb comment written on it: "And Mr. ———— regrets to declare that he will never again review a Peter Drucker book or mention a Peter Drucker article or refer to Peter Drucker in any way, shape or form."[4]

DRUCKER WRITES for professionals, managers, and broadly-educated people from just about everywhere: his books have been translated into at least twenty-five languages. In Whit Stillman's 1994 film, *Barcelona,* the hip young manager played by Taylor Nichols cites

Drucker as gospel to his boss, who listens reverently. Drucker does not fob off on readers like him—smart and ambitious—punctuated tape recordings. He respects his audience too much for that and treats them as his equals in intellectual sophistication. His inclusive "we" invites the reader into his work. In "Reflections of a Social Ecologist," his unexpected term for what he is and does, Drucker says this about his writing:

> For the social ecologist language is doubly important. For language is itself social ecology. For the social ecologist language is not "communication." It is not just "message." It is substance. It is the cement that holds humanity together. It creates community and communion. . . . Social ecologists need not be "great" writers; but they have to be respectful writers, caring writers.

Respectful, caring, yes; but also stylish. Indeed, style is the open secret of the Drucker persuasion, his inimitable fusing of teaching with literary pleasure.[5]

TAKE HIS first sentences. He introduces one of his two novels, *The Last of All Possible Worlds* (1982), puckishly: "This is the first of my 19 books that admits to being fiction." He launches *The Practice of Management* in an appropriately business-like way: "The manager is the dynamic, life-giving element in every business." *The Age of Discontinuity* begins with an act of the historical imagination: "No one knowing only the economic facts and figures of 1968 and of 1913—and ignorant both of the years in between and anything but economic figures—would even suspect the cataclysmic events of this century, the Russian and Chinese Revolutions or the Hitler regime." *The Effective Executive* wastes no time clearing its throat: "To be effective is the job of the executive." *Managing for Results* pours new wine into an old bottle: "This is a 'what-to-do' book." And the opening of a business profile picks a fight: "Everybody knows that Thomas Watson, Sr. (1874–1956) built IBM into a big computer company and was a business leader. But 'everybody' is wrong."[6]

To capture some of the dash of these firsts for his run-of-the-page sentences, Drucker resorts, sparingly but felicitously, to the Homeric epithet, the adjective or adverb that flavors a noun or a verb. He writes, for example, of

"the incurable uncertainty" shrouding all human decisions;
of "the schooled barbarian," the nerd incapable of life;
and of "the swirling chaos of assistants" in the busy office.

Drucker writes that Dr. William Dodd (FDR's first ambassador to Hitler's Germany) notes in his diary, "with incredulous revulsion," that Goebbels has a Ph.D.; that listening to Buckminster Fuller is like splashing in a "verbal Jacuzzi"; that Los Angeles is a "sun-drenched limbo—frowsy palms and peeling stucco"; that in retirement J. P. Morgan drifts into "well-heeled oblivion"; and that commencement speakers are permitted "impassioned twaddle."

Drucker writes dilating sentences in four, "Every product, every process, every technology, every market eventually become old," as well as in three beats: "Top management needs to be known by them, respected by them, accepted by them." His formidable self-confidence expresses itself in epigrammatic flourishes: "It is the nature of knowledge that it changes fast and that today's certainties always become tomorrow's absurdities"; and "The non-profits spend far less for results than governments spend for failure;" and "At least once every five years every form should be put on trial for its life." He has a sardonic voice: "The only profit center is a customer whose check has not bounced." An ironic voice: "Sociology is like acne. Civilization does not die from the disease, but it itches"; and "If only for aesthetic reasons, I am not overfond of the term 'Bottom-Up Management.'"

He even has a poetic voice. Of his grandmother's world, "It smelled of drains and drowned in its own gossip," and "It [innovation] catches, so to speak, the flash of lightning of individual insight that streaks across the horizon, and converts it into permanent light."

What does prose of this quality add to his books? Drucker tells us himself in *The Practice of Management:* "The manager must understand the meaning of the old definition of rhetoric as "the art which draws men's hearts to the love of true knowledge"—Peter Drucker's art of instruction through delight.[7]

YET EVEN Homer nodded. Drucker possesses the defect of his strength, the cultural historian Alan M. Kantrow notes in a perceptive 1980 *Harvard Business Review* essay on Drucker's work. Drucker's penchant for the vivid word—for example, likening the Wall Street traders of the 1980's to "Balkan peasants stealing each other's sheep"—can get the better of his career intention to help readers not only to think clearly but to *see.* "Indeed," Kantrow writes, "it is rhetorically memorable to assert, as Drucker does that 'most sales training is totally unjustified. At best it makes an incompetent salesman out of a moron.' But it also gives heady encouragement to the cavalier dismissal of a perennially knotty problem"—and it is gratuitously insulting to sales people. Drucker the compassionate social ecologist sometimes loses out to Drucker the wielder of the rapier phrase.[8]

As he ages Drucker's paragraphs gather a terse authority: "It [knowledge] is not tied to any country. It is transnational. It is portable. It can be created everywhere, fast and cheaply. Finally, it is, by definition, changing." Also, he does something with the pattern of his paragraphs that is worth stealing. Paragraph one puts forward an unballasted generalization. Paragraph two answers objections to paragraph one, presenting the qualifications and exceptions. Paragraph three develops the generalization from paragraph one in a qualified strength of statement. The order is, A B A. The order A A B would end the paragraph with skepticism, undoing most of the work of A and A. B A A, favored by academics, betrays a lack of confidence. The writer doesn't want *you* to think that *he* hasn't thought of every possible objection to what he has not yet got up the nerve to say.[9]

Mention of Drucker's habit of generalization brings up another characteristic: His penchant for what his beloved Jane Austen called "the *never* of conversation." Examples:

"No totalitarian regime could do *anything* against the will of the masses." Why not the nonoutrageous *"much of anything?"*[10]

"In *every single* business failure in the last few decades, the board was the last to realize that things were going wrong." An "often" after "was" would have saved this from irresponsibility.[11]

"Not a single one," "no one," "every city government"—open a Drucker book (he'd surely say, to "any" page), and stand back for the hyperbole.[12]

Yet another Drucker touch is the arbitrary exactitude of schemas redolent of Chinese Communist agitprop:

The Ten Rules of Effective Research
The Five Telltale Tests of Company Performance
The Five Deadly Business Sins
The Three Popular Explanations
The Two Cores of Unity
The Five Rules of Successful Acquisitions

*One* of his books features: five distinct organization structures, five design principles, three kinds of work, four basic characteristics, four

---

### The Four Different Human Types Needed
### for the Tasks of Top Management

the "thought man"
the "action man"
the "people man"
the "front man"

"Yet those four temperaments are almost never found in one person. . . . The one-man top management job is a major reason why businesses fail to grow."

—*Management: Tasks, Responsibilities, Practices* (1974)

---

questions, three ways, and three different tasks. His schematic confidence extends even beyond the bounds of recorded history: "The aboriginal hunting band had seven to fifteen members."[13]

Here are samples of his medical metaphors:

"Economic satisfactions can be likened to vitamins: their absence creates deficiency diseases of a most serious nature, but they do not in themselves provide calories." (A key Drucker theme, by the way.)

"Keynesian medicine men who inherited their master's prescriptions without having his diagnostic skill are a real menace."

"To vary the metaphor, the mass of modern politics is akin to a massive cancer that overwhelms the human body even though it only weighs a pound." *Vary* the metaphor!

"It [the union] is an anti-organization, an antibody against social toxins." That begins a paragraph this ends: "It [unionism] is a brace needed by a social body suffering from curvature of the spine." Unions go from antibody to brace in a paragraph: Dr. Drucker won't let absurdity keep him from his rounds.[14]

The same book containing the numerical schemas reads in places like a medical journal. Supervisors are the "ligaments, the tendons and sinews of an organization"; specified problems are "the degenerative diseases . . . of the society"; IBM turned the "social disease" of the Depression into an opportunity; the firing-line manager is "the gene of organization in which all higher organs are prefigured"; the effective executive does nothing by half, unlike the surgeon "who takes out only half the tonsils or half the appendix."[15]

These medical moments give the reader the pleasure of anticipation. You keep hoping for rare afflictions or physiologically challenging combinations. That is, if the nonmedical analogue is something like:

*"Both classic and modern economists agree that an adequate monetary system is needed to prevent economic fluctuation from turning into a severe crisis,"* you just know that medical science won't fail Drucker:

*"Otherwise the slightest economic upset, a mere scratch, so to speak, or an attack of the sniffles, turns into deadly worldwide economic collapse, into worldwide economic sepsis or galloping pneumonia."*[16]

A peculiarity of Drucker's books worth mentioning—if only because reviewers sometimes complain about it—is their dearth of footnotes. Drucker, who once told an interviewer that a soap bubble lasts for exactly 25 seconds, is a great one for intellectual improvisation. After attending a Drucker speech, John Tarrant interviewed a man from the packaging industry. "Those statistics [that Drucker had quoted about packaging] are way out of line," the packaging man told Tarrant. He added that Drucker had written about his company in one of his books. "It was very interesting, but, you know, what Drucker said happened was exactly the opposite of what actually did happen." Turning his many source-free pages, the reader can't help wondering, "How does he know all this?" On the rare occasions when the spirit moves him, Drucker tells how by giving a skepticism-shriveling footnote. Thus in *Post-Capitalist Society* (1993) we encounter this starred sentence: "But the first studies of the economic behavior of knowledge have begun to appear."[17] The footnote reads as follows:

*Examples are the work done by Paul Romer of the University of California, Berkeley, such as his two articles "Endogenous Technical Change," in the *Journal of Political Economy* (1990), and "Are Nonconvexities Important for Understanding Growth?" in *American Economic Review* (1990); the work done by Maurice Scott of Oxford, especially his book *A New View of Economic Growth* (Oxford University Press, 1989); and the article by Jacob J. Schwartz, a New York University mathematician and computer scientist, "America's Technological Agenda for the 1990's," in *Daedalus,* the Journal of the American Academy of Arts and Sciences (Winter 1992)—the last a rigorous yet jargon-free presentation of the economics of knowledge-based innovation.

You'd expect this from a young associate professor—it's that level of esoterica. That Drucker keeps up with the very latest work in economic theory is, somehow, moving. It evinces a tenacious will to learn and grow, and not to yield.

AS WE have seen, Drucker swore off predictions after his untimely celebration of the Great Bull Market in 1929. Sometimes he forgets that vow. Even if what's inside these books is not really futurism—and it's not—the titles suggest otherwise: *The Future of Industrial Man; Landmarks of Tomorrow; America's Next Twenty Years; The Frontiers of Management;* and *Managing for the Future.*

The future has wonderfully accommodated Drucker's prescient insights and coinages. In the prefaces written in the early 1990s to Transaction Publishers' editions of his books on society from the 1930s to the 1960s, Drucker rises above false modesty. He was, he tells us, the first to use the concepts "privatization" and "the knowledge society," "among the first" in the early 1950s to imagine the social impact of the computer, "the first observer—in 1961—" to spot the rise of the Japanese economic challenge, "the first to write on Japanese management," the "first to use the term 'post-modern'" (in 1959), the first to write on business strategy, the first to talk of "the society of organizations," and the first to see management as the central organ of that society.[18]

At his best, though, Drucker is not a seer, but a moralist. He is remarkable for his social imagination, not for his futurism. His gift is to explain what is, not to parse wisps of what *could* be.

Drucker's books do not develop arguments, cases, theses, an overarching melody to which the chapters dance. They explore broad topics in chapters that often have no logically necessary link one to another. Those of his books not billed as collections of essays, consequently, read like collections of essays.

Drucker tries to think outside causal chains with their coercive shows of inevitability and their thought-stopping victories. The integrating concept of cause, he writes in *Landmarks of Tomorrow*, is yielding in postmodernity to the concept of configuration. From "Gestalt" to "culture," from "ecology" to "syndrome," science is now establishing and seeking patterns, shapes, configurations—"concepts of the whole." He writes, "We need a discipline that explains events and phenomena in terms of their direction and future state rather than in terms of cause—a calculus of potential, you might say, rather than one of probability." We still lack that discipline; Drucker has been waiting for us to catch up to him for the last forty years. He sees parts not as things that add up one by one to wholes, but as things that exist "in contemplation of the whole." That lovely if puzzling phrase seems to mean: look for the figure in the carpet; don't analyze its chemical composition.

Drucker wants readers to have an "Of course!" reaction to the mix of the new and the familiar in his books. This response, he says, validates his kind of social analysis, which walks the faint line between the known and the unknown. "If such analysis comes up with something people already know, it is likely to be a report on yesterday. If it comes up with something people do not recognize, do not perceive, it is likely to be futuristic, which is euphemism for fairy tale and wishful thinking." Max Weber and Thorstein Veblen, "to name two of the hallowed names," had that "quality of being brand new" and "of course," a suggestive indication of the company Drucker expects to keep on Olympus.[19]

IN HIS *Harvard Business Review* essay Alan Kantrow writes: "Drucker's real contribution to managerial understanding lies not so much in the utility of his ideas as in the rigorous activity of mind by which they are formulated." Drawing from history, philosophy, moral psychology, sociology, politics, science, literature—and, yes, medicine—Drucker's pattern-seeking thinking models how to "identify the constellations of significance in the otherwise chaotic flow of information." His books "enact an unfolding drama of perspective." The drama stems from the openness, the unfoldingness, of his thinking-in-writing. He claims to have "never learned anything from a book"—the Jane Austen "never of conversation." He has to write (or teach) to discover what he thinks. Consequently, his books capture the spontaneity of performances.[20]

And the performances tend toward hope. Because he has spent a good deal of his life studying the one part of American life that *has* to work—business and service-delivering organizations generally—Drucker has no broody pessimism about him. Tough-minded, no pushover for quick fixes, immune to fads, he knows that things can be made to work. Having happened throughout history, innovation—the release of new energies in society, in business, in the nonprofit sector—will happen again.

★　　★　　★

"IN THE TWENTIETH CENTURY the destiny of man ex-
presses itself in political terms," Thomas Mann wrote in the teeth of
the worst the century had to offer. As Drucker says, "It is rash to say
'never' to the future," but that looks as if it will not be true for the
twenty-first century, at least in the postrevolutionary, postsocialist,
even postpolitical West. Robert Teeter, the pollster, charts the dises-
teem of domestic politics in his opinion surveys. "Every person," he
recently told the *New York Times*, "has only so much attention to give
and politics and government takes up only a fraction of what it did
twenty-five years ago. Look at the declining television coverage. Look
at the declining voting rate. Economics and economic news is what
moves the country now." This retreat from politics is most pronounced
among young people. A survey of the 333,000 freshmen entering college in 1994 found less interest and less involvement in politics than in
any freshman class in the 29 years that the poll has been conducted. A
reform movement to drain the Washington swamp and renew the flag-
ging national purpose cannot be ruled out—the Progressive Era followed the Gilded Age, the New Deal the giddy privatism of the 1920s.
But, for this season at any rate, it's hard to see anybody's destiny being
shaped by politics.

In the coming time it's far likelier to be shaped by economic
forces—the lottery of the world market for goods and services and
jobs, the tides of money sloshing through the world financial markets,
technological redundancy, and, generally, the manic pace and intimacy
of change in the information age. Drucker's books are navigational aids
for the new economy.

As if tacitly acknowledging the programmatic hopelessness of
today's single-interest, money-dominated politics, Drucker's latest
books do not depict politics or government as plausible agents of renewal. Drucker is no votary of *laissez-faire,* but his outlook, matching
the evolving public mood, is postpolitical. The really important things

happen beneath politics. When he looks back on the century that is nine years older than he is, the political revolutions and convulsions are not what stand out to him.

> [W]e packed into every decade as much "history" as one usually finds in a century; and little of it was "benign." Yet most of this world, and especially the developed world, somehow managed not only to recover from the catastrophes again and again but to regain direction and momentum—economic, social, even political. The main reason was that ordinary people, people running the every day concerns of business and institutions, took responsibility and kept on building for tomorrow while all around them the world came crashing down.[21]

This is the face the twentieth century will turn tm the twenty-first. Peter Drucker's work will last because it will speak to the continuing world.

# 3

# In Search of the New Society

DRUCKER'S FIRST years in America were decisive in giving direction to his career and contour to his thought. Between 1937 and 1950 Drucker published four major books: *The End of Economic Man* in 1939, *The Future of Industrial Man* in 1942, *The Concept of the Corporation* in 1945, and *The New Society* in 1950. Beginning as a political scientist he ended as Peter Drucker. In these years he discovered the "society of organizations." He became a management consultant. General Motors asked him to take a long inside look at its management. Henry Luce asked him to edit *Fortune*. He and Doris began their family. He took up teaching, his lifetime vocation. He was offered faculty positions at Harvard and Columbia, and he was considered for the deanship of Emory University in Atlanta. (He refused; he would not live in the segregated South.) Happy, increasingly successful, a highly respected writer, sought out by corporations, universities, and governments, Peter Drucker, nevertheless, ended these years in gilded failure. His call to big business and big labor to build an industrial *society* fell on deaf ears. Ignored in America, his vision was embraced in Japan. He became one of the revered American preceptors of Japan's postwar development. Years later, Japanese firms structured on broadly Druckerian lines would overtake the American firms that had ignored him.[1]

Before he could discover the new world, however, Drucker had to finish with the old. Completed in the United States but drafted in Europe, The *End of Economic Man* is a proto-existentialist inquiry into the spiritual and social origins of fascism. More pertinently, *Economic Man* limns a crisis of belief in capitalism (and socialism) whose causes have yet to be ameliorated. Ignoring the specifically German or Italian roots of fascism, Drucker emphasizes civilizational causes. We live in that same civilization.

"This is a political book," Drucker begins. "It has a political purpose: to strengthen the will to maintain freedom against the threat of its abandonment in favor of totalitarianism." Responding warmly to that purpose, Winston Churchill wrote a laudatory review of the book—the first to appear—in the spring of 1939; and, on becoming prime minister in 1940, he ordered it to be included in the "book kit" provided to every graduate of British Officers' Candidate School. "It was, appropriately enough," Drucker wryly notes, "packaged together with Lewis Carroll's *Alice in Wonderland* by somebody in the War Department with a sense of humor."[2]

Drucker begins with blunt criticism of the conventional explanations of fascism. Briefly, these are: fascism is a regression to barbarism, a capitalist ploy to defeat socialism, or the result of propaganda working upon "the gullible masses and their basic instincts." The propaganda argument Drucker calls "the most stupid explanation," because "all means of propaganda were in the hands of uncompromising enemies of fascism during the years of its rise." As for the capitalist ploy, "[I]t is just ridiculous to maintain that the capitalist had any reason to fear a victory of the working classes in pre-fascist Italy and Germany." Relapse into barbarism? A symptom of fascism, not its cause. With sweeping certainty Drucker unveils the true answer: "Fascism is the result of the collapse of Europe's spiritual and social order." "The despair of the masses is the key to understanding fascism," he avers. "No 're-volt of the mob,' no 'triumphs of unscrupulous propaganda,' but the stark despair caused by the breakdown of the old order and the absence of a new one."[3]

The old order that broke down was the reign of *Economic Man*—the personification of the mercantile society organized around the market, the chief "social institution of the nineteenth century," the economy of market towns that forms the background to the Wessex novels of Thomas Hardy. That society saw as its purpose "the establishment of freedom and justice through economic development," as Drucker phrases it elsewhere. But economic freedom under the market did not lead to social justice or equality. Quite the opposite. Thus, the "failure to establish equality by economic freedom has destroyed the belief in capitalism as a social system." And the goalposts of freedom and equality are immovable. "With Christianity, freedom and equality became the two basic concepts of Europe; they are themselves Europe." In the age of *Economic Man* the more of the former there was, however, the less of the latter. This breach between social promise and social fact defined the crisis of the old order.[4]

---

### Fascism's Noneconomic Society

"Since the masses had lost their faith in economic progress, they would not have been willing to make the necessary sacrifices in consumption for the sake of economically productive investment. They could not have been persuaded or forced to forgo present satisfactions in order to obtain greater *economic* satisfactions in the distant future. The sacrifices had to be imposed for the sake of a noneconomic goal. Fascist society has to be noneconomic, its goal the military autarchy of *Wehrwirtschaft*."

—*The End of Economic Man* (1939)

If capitalism was no longer belief-worthy, socialism was ideologi-
cally bankrupt. The socialist Arcadia of the universal brotherhood of
man ended on the same August day in 1914 when young Peter
Drucker eavesdropped on history. "On that day it was shown that the
solidarity of interests and of beliefs between the labor movement and
the capitalist society of each country is stronger than the international
solidarity of the working class. . . . The proletarian masses, that great
powerful force for peace and brotherhood, everywhere ignited like tin-
der in a patriotic firestorm." Its dream of a classless and stateless world
in embers, socialism has ceased to be an alternative economic system to
capitalism, becoming "a mere opposition within capitalism."[5]

The Great War and the Great Depression made this engulfing crisis of belief a felt reality for millions. "These catastrophes broke
through the everyday routine which makes men accept existing forms,
institutions and tenets as unalterable natural laws. They suddenly exposed the vacuum behind the facade of society." Fascism filled that

---

### On Capitalism

"Capitalism as a social order and as a creed is the expression of the belief
in economic progress as leading toward the freedom and equality of the individual in a free and equal society. Marxism expects this society to result from
the abolition of private profit. Capitalism expects the free and equal society
to result from the enthronement of private profit as supreme ruler of social
behavior. . . .

"There is an unbroken chain of opposition to the introduction of economic freedom and to the capitalist autonomy of the economic sphere. . . .
In every case the opposition could only be overcome—peacefully or by
force—because of the promise of capitalism to establish equality. . . . That
this promise was an illusion we all know."

— The End of Economic Man (1939)

vacuum with magic. Robbed of belief in the justice and rationality of the social order, the masses

> ... must turn their hopes toward a miracle. In the depths of their despair reason cannot be believed, truth must be false, and lies must be truth. "Higher bread prices," "lower bread prices," "unchanged bread prices" have all failed. The only hope lies in a kind of bread price which is none of these, which nobody has ever seen before, and which belies the evidence of one's reason.

*Economic Man*'s longest chapter introduces a theme that Drucker will touch on in book after book: Fascism's attempt to create a "noneconomic society." He calls it "fascism's social miracle."

Fascism needed a miracle to mask its economic failure. In a series of articles he wrote for *The Banker,* a trade journal, and published in a book *Germany—The Last Four Years,* under the pen name "Germanicus," Drucker gave an authoritative analysis of the state-controlled German economy. To finance the "most gigantic arms production program ever undertaken," the economy had been driven into the ground. Issuing 700 to 1000 economic directives every week, the six-level-deep Nazi bureaucracy required businessmen to fill out as many as 600 forms to complete foreign trade deals. The Nazi planners wrecked German agriculture to the point where, as early as January 1937, rationing had to be introduced. With daily caloric intake falling, with unemployment kept from catastrophic levels only by "Defence Economics," the Nazis devised a system of noneconomic satisfactions and incentives—for example, furnishing the lower classes with "some of the noneconomic paraphernalia of economic privilege," theater tickets, winter cruises, stays at health spas. During the workday Hans may have been a lowly janitor, but after work he was a somebody in the Nazi Party. "The son of the 'boss' or the boss himself is intentionally put under one of the unskilled laborers who has been longer in the party." Noneconomic motives and satisfactions would be a major emphasis of Drucker's later work. Strange to say, but fascism's social miracle is at the back of his mind in assessing American society.[6]

For all its insight, you need a high tolerance for the fleshless progress of abstractions to wholly admire *Economic Man*. Drucker typically pins a name on something without empirically observable existence—Spiritual Man, Intellectual Man, Economic Man, Heroic Man, Free and Equal Man. Then he treats these lexical triumphs with all the courtesy due realities. Brilliant, original, intellectually intrepid, *The End of Economic Man* is still the book of a young man who does not yet trust his own powers of observation. Instead of interpreting realities, he posits them. America will bring out the strength of his mind—his pragmatic yet value-seeking intelligence.

With William James the mature Drucker asks, What is the "cash-value" of an idea; what are its results? In his books he is scornful of the sleek pleasers who only talk a good game. Performance is the only fair test. His pragmatism increasingly asserts itself not as doctrine but as temperament. Instinctively, he is hostile to *a priori* world views, philosophical systems, political ideologies, visions of perfection, "salvation by society," plans for Utopia. As he gets older his views dapple; he is more at home with a world unredeemed by ideas, with the mixed verdicts of experience, with ambiguity and "workable imperfection." In party politics Drucker is a "mugwump," who splits his vote "at least once—and often four different ways." In political philosophy he calls himself an "old conservative." "Like [Walter] Bagehot," he writes of a figure close to him in intellectual deportment, "I see as central to society and to civilization the tension between the need for continuity (Bagehot called it 'the cake of custom') and the need for innovation and change." This makes him a man of the political middle. "Thus, I know what Bagehot meant when he said that he saw himself as a liberal Conservative and sometimes as a conservative Liberal but never as a 'conservative Conservative' or a 'liberal Liberal.'" Never believing for a moment in Marxism and regarding Russian Communism as morally indistinguishable from fascism (as George Orwell noted in an essay), Drucker does not have to prove his attachment to democratic capitalism. He is for it, not out of secular theology, like many contemporary conservatives; rather, because, with all its social injustices and environmental depredations, capitalism works. And so, within its limits, does government. "No matter how deeply wedded one may be to the free enterprise system (and I, for one, am wedded for life)," he wrote in 1957, "one has to accept the need for positive government; one has to consider government action on a sizable scale as desirable rather than a necessary evil." He expressed the same underlying thought in an *Atlantic Monthly* essay in 1994. The consistency is less admirable than Drucker's long espousal of the view. It is one thing for John Kenneth Galbraith to write that government action is desirable, it is another for Peter Drucker, whose core readers are corporate executives. To speak truth as you see it in all seasons is intellectual integrity, and from first to last Drucker's work is a well of that rare quality.[7]

DRUCKER GOT his first American job in 1939 as a part-time teacher of economics at Sarah Lawrence College in Bronxville, New York, where the Druckers made their first home in America. They were not made to feel at home, however. Fellow travelers with the Soviet Union were thick on the ground among the Sarah Lawrence faculty, as Drucker painfully discovered. "I was then (Spring of '41) the only member of the faculty who refused to sign a communist manifesto which viciously and falsely attacked the liberal president of Brooklyn College, Harry Gideonse," Drucker writes in "Political Correctness and American Academe." At a time when the party line was to support Hitler, President Gideonse had dared to call for support of Britain in its stand-alone war with Hitler. In addition, he had prevented a takeover of his faculty by "a communist front organization." For refusing to sign his name to the faculty's anathema on Gideonse, Drucker was fired. He had seen this intolerance of mental independence before—in Frankfurt, under Nazi rule.[8]

He quickly found a new teaching job at Bennington College in Vermont. The war on, as he relates in *Adventures of a Bystander,* he also became a part-time consultant, on international economic policy, to the Board of Economic Warfare. Earlier, he had been rejected for military service on account of poor eyesight. He says of his wartime contribution: "I was a utility outfielder. . . . I was brought in to do things in which I was totally dispensable." Though surrounded by military solemnity, he kept his wit intact. Shortly after Pearl Harbor he was living and working in a converted Washington apartment hotel with other civilian knowledge workers. One day, amid military punctilio, a colonel appeared with a package marked Top Secret. "After he had left, we opened with great trepidation the bundle he had brought and found a book inside: the first intelligence study of a European country. Then we read the opening sentence: 'The Estonians are by nature monogamous,' and collapsed in laughter."[9]

Bennington College had a distinguished faculty in the early 1940s. Erich Fromm, the writer and psychoanalyst, taught there; as did (thanks to Drucker) the famed economic historian Karl Polanyi; and—Martha Graham. Invariably a sheltered young woman, one of Drucker's student advisees, would come up to him at the start of term and shyly inquire, "Mr. Drucker, what is a 'cunt'?" The Vesuvian Graham had held her first class in modern dance.[10]

BETWEEN SARAH Lawrence and Bennington Drucker began talking out his next book. He teaches, he says, in order to find out what he thinks. Although crucial chapters were written "in the summer of 1940 when the radio every day blared out news of Nazi victories," *The Future of Industrial Man* looks past the headlines to outline a new social vision for the postwar world. Written after Europe went to war in September 1939 and finished before Pearl Harbor, *The Future of Industrial Man* was published in early 1942. Its dramatic themes resound in these uncompromising dicta:

> "No social power can endure unless it is legitimate power."
>
> "Unless the power in the corporation can be organized on an accepted principle of legitimacy, it will . . . be taken over by a central government . . ."
>
> "Unless the members of the industrial system are given the social status and function they lack today, our society will disintegrate."
>
> "We have only one alternative: either to build a functioning industrial society or to see freedom itself disappear in anarchy and tyranny."[11]

Reviews ranged from the laudatory to the scornful. In the *New Republic* the eminent cultural historian Jacques Barzun wrote: "Here is a book so perfectly planned and so transparently written as to read with almost indecent ease. . . . Each page is the fruit of much learning and long reflection. It should accordingly be studied, pondered over, analyzed word by word." In the *Yale Review,* the *New York Times* editorial writer Henry Hazlitt confessed himself at a loss to fathom Drucker's "specialized, private vocabulary." "Mr. Drucker may have precise concepts behind such labels as 'mercantile,' 'industrial,' 'status,' 'function,' 'freedom,' 'totalitarian,' but he never makes clear what those concepts are. He gives his own meaning to words."[12]

"Reviewers of Mr. Drucker's work habitually use the word 'brilliant.' Let us admit it: Mr. Drucker is 'brilliant.' But:

There is a curious combination in his style of a Germanic mysticism and a popular-magazine looseness that is fatal to any precision of thought. Reading Mr. Drucker is like driving with bright headlights on through an intermittent fog. For a moment, the road ahead seems clear. One strikes the fog: the headlights are still on: there is, certainly, illumination. But it is merely a brilliant blur.

That is very wide of justice. But Drucker was still writing as a political scientist, which accounts for a good deal of the fog; and he had yet to find the wise man's voice familiar to millions from his later books.

IN THE *End of Economic Man* Drucker warned of applying its conclusions to the U.S. "Whatever the underlying forces are which will determine the developments in the United States, they are different from those in Europe." *The Future of Industrial Man* drops that caveat. In the middle of a war against Germany, when it took extraordinary mental freedom to think beyond the black and white of propaganda, he warns that the U.S. is not exempt from the forces that made fascism:

> Unless we realize that the essence of Nazism is also an attempt to solve a universal problem of Western civilization—that of the industrial society—and that the basic principles on which the Nazis base this attempt are also in no way confined to Germany, we do not know what we fight for or what we fight against. . . . The war is being fought for the structure of industrial society—its basic principles, its purposes, and its institutions.[13]

We *are* of the same civilization. "Totalitarianism grew out of a collapse of values, beliefs, and institutions common to all Western countries." World War II is "a civil war for the future of Western society."

Fascism, he says in *Economic Man,* "can only deny the concept of Economic Man which has broken down. It cannot create the new concept which should take its place. But unless a new order and a new concept based upon the European values of freedom and equality can be found, Europe and the Occident are doomed." Would the new society be organized around slavery and war, or around freedom and equality? The future of Industrial Man hung on the answer.[14]

Drucker begins *Industrial Man* where he left off in *Economic Man:* we are in no-man's land without a concept to fit our new reality. Economic Man is dead and Industrial Man is struggling to be born. Though the market thrives as an economic mechanism, the mercantile society organized around the market is gone. A new institution has appeared to assume the market's central social place—the industrial corporation. So has a new social form—the assembly-line system of mass production. But industrialism has not advanced beyond these rudiments. It has thus far failed to create an industrial society, the "new order" and "new concept" based on freedom and equality without which we are "doomed." This invocation of the apocalypse raises fearfully the intellectual stakes on Drucker's proposed solutions. What steps *can be taken* to head off "doom"?

"No society can function as a society," Drucker postulates, not argues, "unless it gives the individual member social status and function,

---

### On Freedom

"Political freedom is neither easy nor automatic, neither pleasant nor secure. It is the responsibility of the individual for the decisions of society as if they were his own decisions—as in moral truth and accountability they indeed are."

—*The Future of Industrial Man* (1942)

and unless the decisive social power is legitimate." Materialists may doubt that societies have aims or purposes, properties usually thought to belong exclusively to persons. Drucker, they may feel, has not yet been weaned from German Idealism. Hegel read mind into State; Drucker reads it into Society. Fair enough. But let's stay with Drucker's argument before we argue with its premises.[15]

What would a functioning society look like? First of all its members would have "status" within that society. As Hazlitt noted, this is to use 'status' in a different-seeming sense from its ordinary meaning. Drucker never satisfactorily pins this new meaning down for the reader. He cites a famous contrast made by Ferdinand Toennies, the German sociologist: "Toennies juxtaposed community, which is focused on being, that is status, with society, which is focused on doing, that is function." But dragging in the incurably vague "being" doesn't help matters. Although put through the ontological hoops, in the end status does have for Drucker something of its quotidian meaning. "Status" is partly our sense of belonging to a society, partly what we mean when we speak of our *place* in society, and partly our place as recognized and accepted by other members of the society. While our status is not "fixed," it is "definite." Drucker splits this hair to distinguish the Hindu caste system from mobile societies.[16]

"Function" is one's role in society. Tinker, tailor, soldier, spy: these are social roles. If you are unemployed, you lose your function. If this continues, your sense of belonging will also erode to the point where you also lose your place—your status. The collapse of all morale among people long unemployed implicates more than economics. To lose status and function, in everyday language, "individual dignity and personal fulfillment," is to lose the showing parts of one's identity. Evocatively, in language reminiscent of Albert Camus' *The Stranger*, Drucker describes man in the social wilderness:

He sees only demoniac forces, half sensible, half meaningless, half in light and half in darkness, but never predictable. . . . He is like a blindfolded man in a strange room, playing a game of which he does not know the rules; and the prize at stake is his own happiness, his own livelihood, and even his own life.

Finally, legitimacy. For Drucker this concept retains its ordinary meaning. "Legitimate is a power when it is justified by an ethical or metaphysical principle that has been accepted by the society." Illegitimate power is "might" not "authority." In a functioning society power is exercised as authority—power made right by common assent.

Turning from these semantic toils, we now see what Drucker means when he says that the new industrial system, defined by the corporation and mass production, had yet to become an industrial *society*. Status and function "makes comprehensible and rational individual existence from the point of the group, and group existence from that of the individual." Nobody would apply this benediction to the assembly-line worker under mass production. Drucker yields nothing to the young Marx on the existential wretchedness of the alienated worker:

> *Marx:* "The alienation of the worker in his product means not only that his labor becomes an object, something that exists outside of him . . . it means that the life he has conferred on the object confronts him as something hostile and alien."
>
> *Drucker:* "Work appears as something unnatural, a disagreeable, meaningless and stultifying condition . . . devoid of dignity as well as of importance. [The worker] is not a human being in society, but a freely replaceable cog in an inhumanly efficient machine."

And these insults to dignity and individuality are not the end of it. There is also a political insult. The power wielded over the worker in the large corporate entity lacks warrants of legitimacy. The owners, whose property rights established their legitimacy in the old-time firm, no longer own the corporation. The stockholders don't effectively own it, either; they rarely concern themselves with it, and they are too various to act in concert on anything short of screaming managerial incompetence. In a passage of unmasking candor, reminiscent of Freud's unmasking of the unconscious in everyday life and of Marx's unmasking of the fetish of commodities, Drucker lays bare an historic usurpation of power:

> In the modern corporation the decisive power, that of the managers, is derived from no one but from the managers themselves controlled by nobody and nothing and responsible to no one. It is in the most literal sense unfounded, unjustified, uncontrolled and irresponsible power.[17]

Drucker rejects the then-influential idea advanced by James Burnham ("and the managers who applauded him") in *The Managerial Revolution* that "actual rule simply creates its own ideological justification." The "evidence," he says, counters this claim. Because most Americans still accept the standard of Economic Man that property rights establish legitimacy, he argues, they backed Henry Ford, sole owner of his company, in his fight against unions and the New Deal in the 1930s. But no such "popular support" was extended to General Motors, the professionally managed company *par excellence*. GM's "actual rule" was not enough to justify its right to rule. This "evidence" hardly settles the matter. Drucker rarely cites public opinion polls or the like to ballast his arguments.

Drucker's vision of society, to bring it down a peg, recalls Garrett Fitzgerald, the former Irish prime minister, known for saying of a thing, that it's all very well in practice, but how does it sound in theory? Drucker wants industrial society to sound good in *his* theory. That its institutions more or less work in practice is not enough for him (although it *will* be enough: by the late 1960s "justification by performance" becomes his test of legitimacy). He measures reality by its conformance to the Idea. Further, he applies sociological concepts (status, function) and concepts from political science (legitimacy) to economic quiddities like the corporation and mass production. But he does not mount a philosophical argument to justify these and only these categories as truth's vessels. Socially attractive, morally appealing, intuitively desirable, status, function, and legitimacy remain Druckerian impositions.

Still, in Drucker's world they stand for the humanistic conviction that economy must serve community and society—people first, commodities a close second. If that conviction is worldless idealism, one wants very much to say, then so much the worse for the world. Drucker holds the glass of the possible up to the actual. And a society that respects human dignity *is* possible.

While other commentators feared that wartime regimentation was a preview of postwar totalitarianism, Drucker saw the war as "a tremendous opportunity for constructive political action" toward the new society of Industrial Man. "The War offers precisely what our society has been lacking: a social function and status for the individual, and a common social purpose for society."

As a concrete example, he cites the making of war planes. One manufacturer increased mechanization of work *and* increased morale by using his imagination. He had the people who flew the planes take through the planes the people who built them: here is where the part you installed fits in, and here is why putting it in right is a vital job. Take the evidence from Britain: "According to all observers, the war brought the industrial worker a satisfaction, a feeling of importance and achievement, a certainty of citizenship, self-respect and pride. . . ." Yet this was the very sort of assembly-line work that left workers be-

---

**On Bureaucracy**

"There is no greater mistake than to take the politics out of government. If it is done by making a civil service bureaucracy omnipotent and by entrusting political decisions to the expert selected by the merit system of competitive examinations, it leads not only to the government of the least fit but straight to the tyranny of the printed form."

—*The Future of Industrial Man* (1942)

---

fore the war feeling like so many "cogs." The difference was not in the industrial technique—the same in both cases—but in the social circumstances of production. The assembly line is far less alienating for the worker when he sees how his contribution fits into the whole and when, more importantly, his work is invested with high social purpose.

Drucker is here at his most visionary. To avoid the "moral depression" that poisoned the lees of the first war, he concludes, Americans must find in the social tonic of the war—"the wartime integration of individual and group, the wartime unity of purpose and belief"—a pattern for the new society. As for the fear of postwar totalitarianism, that was a hobgoblin. Americans loved freedom too much. The wartime dignity and social meaning in even menial work: that was the thing to hold on to. "But how does one endow can openers or lamp shades with social meaning and purpose?" he would ask eight years later in *The New Society*. There lay the unprecedented social challenge of peacetime, for "the worker demands . . . after the experience of the War that his work be meaningful."[18]

Drucker, then, has established why the industrial system of peacetime is not an industrial *society*. An industrial society would give the worker status and function. It would make his employer's power legitimate in his eyes. And it would make his work meaningful. The stage is set for a clash between these humanistic ideals and corporate realities.

# 4

# Inside GM

IN THE wake of *Industrial Man,* picture Drucker as U. S. Grant lolling in the general store in Galena, waiting for the call of destiny. "I came to the conclusion in the book," Drucker told Warren Bennis in an interview, "that we're living in a society of organizations and I needed to know something about them. I knew nothing then." And, from a different interview,

> I decided that I needed to be inside, to really study a big company from the inside: as a human, social, political organization—as an integrating mechanism. I tried to get inside, and I had met a few people as a journalist and as an investment banker. They all turned me down. The chairman of Westinghouse was very nice to me when I came to see him, but when I told him what I wanted he not only threw me out, he gave instructions to his staff not to allow me near the building because I was a Bolshevik.[1]

Bennis asked Drucker how he first got involved with management:

> I slid into consulting, or fell into it. I got a telephone call, out of the blue, around Christmas 1943. We had moved to New York for the winter from Bennington . . . I had come to the conclusion that I needed to study a major institution. . . . I had almost given it up when I got the telephone call and a man said, "My name is Paul Garrett. I'm vice president for

Public Relations of General Motors calling on behalf of the corporation's vice chairman Mr. Donaldson Brown. Mr. Brown wonders whether you might be interested in making a study of General Motors' policies and structure for the company's top management. . . ." When I got this GM assignment at Christmas, I needed money. But above all it was exactly the kind of study I needed badly for my own sake. . . . It was literally, for me, the finger of providence.[2]

Drucker's first two books had launched him promisingly in political science: the American Political Science Association had even elected him to its committee on political-theory research. The GM project, however, was afield from political science. Lewis Jones, the president of Bennington College, described the risk Drucker was running in jumping the academic rails. "You are going to destroy your career in academia forever. You are now at the point where you can go into economics or into political science. With this topic you will lose all respectability in either." ("He was absolutely right," Drucker says.) Established disciplines would sniff at a study of a profit-making institution—only the world's largest corporation. Worse, there was no other discipline, no field of knowledge, to which the GM project belonged. A survey of books at the New York Public Library on corporate management turned up virtually nothing. "I am ashamed to admit how little I knew about management. It was amazing, not because I was so ignorant, but because *nobody* knew anything."[3]

In reading *The Future of Industrial Man*, GM's Donaldson Brown thought he saw a kindred spirit in Drucker: his preoccupation with corporate governance and the role of business in society resonated with the concerns of GM executives planning for the postwar world. Drucker's assignment was to write an in-house report. Directly, Drucker found this wouldn't work: GM people treated him like a spy for top management. "Nobody wants to talk to me," he reported to Brown.

> *Brown:* Is there any way we can straighten it out?
>
> *Drucker:* Yes, it's quite easy. All we have to do is to tell them I'm writing a book, because everybody in this country will do anything for a writer.
>
> *Brown:* I'm almost 60, and I have never lied to any of my associates and I won't start now.
>
> *Drucker* (stunned): If you are not willing to let me say that I think it's going to be very difficult.
>
> Brown deliberated a week.
>
> *Brown:* I made a few checks and you are right. But I will not let you say anything that is not true. So the Executive Committee has authorized me to let you write a book.
>
> *Drucker:* I hope you'll edit it to make sure there's nothing in it that you find very offensive.
>
> *Brown:* I don't believe in censorship. We will read it for factual errors. Period.

Brown doubted the book's prospects. "I don't see anyone interested in a book on management," he said. (Initially, Drucker's publisher agreed: "Who the hell wants to know how a big company is organized?") Brown's notion of the book market (about 2,000 business books are now published every year) seems as antique as his aspect of Roman integrity. That was a quality esteemed at GM. The one definition of what makes an executive at GM that Drucker could find was, "A man who would be expected to protest officially against a policy decision to which he objects." Yet these same principled men ran a company that, as recently as the late 1930s, had been the country's leading employer of labor spies, whom it used to root out union sympathizers from its plants; a company that had used violence against sit-down strikers putting their bodies on the line for the right to organize; a company, in short, with a hard past. As events will show, neither labor nor management could escape it.[4]

If Brown was chilling in his scrupulosity, Alfred P. Sloan was rectitude incarnate. The famed chairman of the board of GM was a sort of corporate monk. Nobody ever saw his wife, and he had no children. He lived, Drucker says, in "a cubicle in General Motors' dormitory in Detroit; it didn't even have a private bathroom. He had a bedroom on the Detroiter and a similar cubicle in the General Motors offices in New York. He rarely used his apartment on Fifth Avenue and he had an estate on Long Island where I think he went for Christmas. . . ." Yet throughout the executive precincts of GM, Sloan was known as the man to see if you were in trouble. He gave up most of one Christmas vacation, according to an emblematic story Drucker tells in his introduction to Sloan's autobiography, "to find the hospital where the badly burnt child of a plant manager could get the best medical care—and he had never even met the plant manager."[5]

Slight, with a long face and white hair and wearing a hearing aid with a big trumpet protruding from his bad ear, "Mr. Sloan," to all at GM, did not look formidable. On their first meeting, however, Drucker saw why Sloan had moral authority to spare among his executives. "You have probably heard, Mr. Drucker," he began, "that I didn't initiate your study. I saw no point to it. My associates overruled me. It is therefore my duty to make sure that you can do the best job you are capable of. Come and see me any time I can be of help." The chairman was not a man to tell the socially lubricating lie.

In *The Effective Executive* (1966) Drucker recreates Sloan speaking at that first meeting. "The executive thinking through a decision," Drucker says, "might put this in front of him in neon lights."

I shall not tell you what to write, what to study, or what conclusions to come to. This is your task. My only instruction to you is to put down what you think is right as you see it. Don't you worry about our reaction . . . And don't you, above all, concern yourself with the compromises that might be needed to make your recommendations acceptable. There is not one executive in this company who does not know how to make every single conceivable compromise without any help from you. But he can't make the "right" compromises unless you first tell him what "right" is.[6]

In *Adventures of a Bystander* Drucker brings Alfred P. Sloan to life. Asked to name "the perfect management tool," Drucker typically replies, "Alfred Sloan's hearing aid." When Sloan turned it on or off, "it sounded like the crack of doom," riveting the room on him. When he took a position the facts did not support, he would quickly reverse himself, saying, "The facts have made the decision—I was wrong." This was management by moral example, and it greatly influenced Drucker, who would teach two generations of executives to lead by action not exhortation.[7]

Sitting in on a meeting of GM executives, Drucker was struck by the time spent discussing the job of one master mechanic. After the meeting he sought out Sloan: "Mr. Sloan, how can you afford to spend four hours on a minor job like that?"

---

### Alfred P. Sloan's Executive Credo

" 'Some people like to be alone,' he said; 'I don't. I have always liked good company. But I have a duty not to have friends at the work place. I have to be impartial and must not give the impression of having favorites. How people perform, that is my job; whether I approve of them and the way they get their achievement done, is not.' He never gave an opinion on a person, only on his performance."

—*Adventures of a Bystander* (1979)

"This corporation pays me a pretty good salary for making important decisions, and for making them right," Sloan replied. "Some of us up here at the fourteenth floor may be very bright; but if that master mechanic in Dayton is the wrong man, our decisions might as well be written on water. He converts them into performance."

Taking out his "famous little black book," Sloan did a rapid calculation. GM had forty-seven divisions. In the previous year, top management made "people decisions" on 143 jobs in those divisions. That worked out to three per division, a bearable load. "If we didn't spend four hours on placing a man and placing him right," he told Drucker, "we'd spend four hundred hours cleaning up after our mistakes." Decisions on people, Sloan said, were the most important decisions an executive could make, giving Drucker an enduring lesson in management.[8]

DRUCKER SPENT eighteen months researching and writing *Concept of the Corporation,* visiting every GM division and most GM plants east of the Mississippi. He attended board meetings, met all the top people at GM, and interviewed workers on the shop floor. With the war still on, GM's plants had been converted to war production—the company did not make a single car between October 1942 and September 1945—and this circumstance colors the book. Drucker saw beyond the actuality of the assembly line to its possibility: high morale, increased productivity, enhanced worker initiative and responsibility, meaningful work. However, Drucker made these observations at Potemkin factories. Over a hundred thousand GM employees served in the war; to replace them and to fill the War Department's Niagara of contracts GM hired 750,000 new employees, of whom 30 percent were women. The employees he saw working with such high morale not only had the unique motivation of wartime patriotism; they were new to factory work, at least under the GM system, and the work itself was stimulatingly novel—making tanks and planes and machine guns—not cars. With the wartime instability, people flitted in and out of jobs; at full employment, they were easy to find. Thus Drucker got little chance to observe the factory "lifer," the twenty-year prisoner of the GM plant. Lifers had worked for GM before the war as they would after. The war, the fresh workers, the gender of many of them, and the novelty of the work—these features of wartime mass-production inevitably distorted his vision, lending it a Panglossian flavor. His transformative hopes for the postwar era rested on illusory grounds.

Drucker finds his voice in this book.

Of the busy executive: "Problems have to be presented to him in a form which allows him to act, that is, stripped of everything not pertaining to the business of the moment."

Of the corporation: "To borrow a metaphor from modern psychology, an institution is like a tune; it is not constituted by individual sounds but by the relations between them."

Of profit: "Profit is . . . the basis of all economic activity, whether capitalist, socialist or caveman." And surely only Peter Drucker would describe a General Motors as *an essay in federalism.*"[9]

*CONCEPT OF THE CORPORATION* was published in November 1945, just as the United Automobile Workers (UAW) went out on strike against GM. The timing was inauspicious for a book advocating a new era of cooperation between labor and management. As we will see, the Drucker book called for major changes in GM's employee relations. GM, however, was bent on restoring the prewar status quo. The UAW had called the GM strike to set the terms of the emergent industrial society of the postwar era. As, in *Fortune*'s words, "the world's most influential industrial unit in forming the life patterns of the machine age," GM sought very different terms.[10]

> ### On Decentralization
>
> "Decentralization, as the term is usually understood, means division of labor and is nothing new. . . . But in General Motors usage, decentralization is much more than that. In over twenty years of work, first from 1923 to 1937 as President, since then as Chairman of the Corporation, Mr. Alfred P. Sloan Jr. has developed the concept of decentralization into a philosophy of industrial management and into a system of local self-government. It is not a mere technique of management but an outline of a social order."
>
> —*Concept of the Corporation* (1945)

CONCEPT OF THE CORPORATION is famous in management circles for introducing "decentralization" as a principle of organization. "By the 1980s," John Micklethwait and Adrian Wooldridge write in *The Witch Doctors,* a lively guide to management thinkers, "Drucker was credited with moving 75–80 percent of the *Fortune* 500 to radical decentralization."[11]

Since Alfred P. Sloan became its president in the 1920s, General Motors had been a decentralized corporation, its many divisions enjoying considerable autonomy from central management. About 95 percent of all decisions, Drucker found, "fell within the jurisdiction" of the division managers. Central management set car prices, negotiated labor contracts, furnished the capital, and did much of the paper work. But the divisional management of Oldsmobile, for example, could buy car accessories from a non-GM distributor—or do nearly anything else. "[C]entral management refrains as much as possible from telling a division how to do its job; it only lays down what to do."

Of course actual performance sometimes fell short of this standard. Drucker was in the office of an executive at GM's Detroit headquarters listening to the man's "favorite sermon on the beatitudes of decentralization" when the office teleprinter noisily coughed up a message. "Pay no attention," the executive said. "It's only the Kansas City plant manager letting me know he's going to lunch," and continued his sermon on the freedom enjoyed by local managers."[12]

For Drucker, who calls his chapter on decentralization "The Corporation as Human Effort," the human side of the policy was cardinal. Young executives got their feet wet in the divisions before moving up to central management, making their mistakes where mistakes were either correctable or not company-threatening. With the big-company safety net beneath them, they could display their entrepreneurial talents. And, given real authority, they weren't likely to retire on the job or quit out of boredom and frustrated ambition. The ever-flattening corporate managements of the 1990s leave Drucker concerned that the leadership-development purpose of decentralization is in process of being lost. The flat organization does not permit managerial farm teams.

The connection between managerial ambition and decentralization leads Drucker to see unusual social value today in "unbundling" or "outsourcing," the controversial practice through which big organizations subcontract nonessential tasks to smaller firms specializing in them. Drucker's example is from hospital management. Cleaning workers are at the bottom of the hospital's steep hierarchy. Outsourced cleaners hired by the hospital to do the same work are not at the bottom. In their companies' short hierarchies they are only one or two jobs removed from being foremen, supervisors, or managers themselves. "The productivity of service work is not likely to go up until it is possible to be promoted for doing a good job at it," Drucker says. But more than efficiency is involved. "Outsourcing is necessary because it provides opportunities, income, and dignity for service workers," Drucker writes in *Post-Capitalist Society* (1993).[13]

Outsourcing is the kind of social innovation Drucker strongly encourages not to save money or to increase efficiency, but to help capitalism keep its promise of equal opportunity. Efficiency is not a major Drucker goal. "The last buggy whip factory was no doubt a model of efficiency" is a characteristic swipe at the accountant's vision. Drucker wants work to reflect social values like opportunity, community, solidarity, and individual fulfillment, not just business values like cost and efficiency.[14]

*Concept of the Corporation* is a book about business as *Moby-Dick* is a book about whaling. Barely a third of its 330 pages deal frontally with GM's policies and management. The rest touches on GM only as the hook for a larger discussion about the corporation as a social institution and about economic policy in the postwar era. Here is an outline of Drucker's argument:

• The corporation is the "representative institution" of the era. "Only now have we realized that the large mass-production plant is our social reality . . . which has to carry the burden of our dreams."

• Those dreams are American dreams of equality of opportunity and personal achievement.

• More people can realize more of these dreams in an industrial society than ever before in history. This is primarily because the industrial system requires whole new categories of skilled workers—from managers to technicians—that did not exist a generation before. Industrialism creates its own middle class.

• Yet, according to surveys of public opinion, most Americans see opportunities narrowing under the great industrial corporations. The new relation of school to work is chiefly to blame. Long schooling reflects the financial position of one's family. Opportunities for advancement are seen to go to the already advanced. This "puts into question the promise to youth to be judged on performance" rather than by genetic luck and thus is rightly seen as "a substantial weakness of the industrial system and . . . a substantial failure to fulfill the promises of our society."

• Another reason most Americans do not yet see opportunities expanding under the industrial corporation is that "getting ahead" has only an economic meaning in America. This leads to dissatisfaction, since there are not enough jobs to really "get ahead" in. We need noneconomic criteria for success; otherwise the system will continue to affront dignity and destroy self-respect.

• Admittedly it's hard to square dignity and self-respect with mass production on the assembly line. Fortunately war production has shown alternatives—even efficient ones—to Charlie Chaplin's caricature in *Modern Times*. Monotony and rigid specialization are incidental, not essential, features of industrialism. Drucker has long been critical of the assembly line. "I have always called it 'bad engineering' precisely because it does not build on the specifically *human* strengths and equally because it makes the strength of one worker a threat to all others."[15]

GM'S TOP executives might have indulged Drucker's eloquent pleas to live up to the possible. But Drucker's calls for GM to lead America into the new industrial society could not have been welcome. Indeed, with the Westinghouse CEO who ordered Drucker off the premises, GM's executives could be forgiven for regarding Drucker as a Viennese variety of Bolshevik.

Drucker called for fundamental change. Industry should count workers as a resource, not a cost. Workers should play a role in governing the workplace in the "self-governing plant community." Full *private-sector* employment should be the first economic priority of the postwar. Finally, and most controversially, corporations like GM should pay *a guaranteed annual wage* to their long-term workers. This would allow families to maintain something like their normal standard of living (the guaranteed wage would be a contractually determined percentage of the worker's salary) during layoffs caused by dips in the business cycle for which they were in no way to blame. Industrial citizenship, which following the political model implied rights and responsibilities, demanded no less. This is what it meant to treat workers as a resource. Drucker also defended guaranteed wages on macroeconomic grounds: If laid-off workers could still collect a generous share of their salaries during economic slumps, their uninterrupted purchasing power would hasten recovery. Walter Reuther, unfortunately for Drucker, was making much the same argument.

DRUCKER HAD not gone completely "Bolshie." He penned one of his first panegyrics to profit as the irreplaceable economic precondition of industrial society. On the conservative ground of preserving free enterprise, he wanted companies given tax incentives to encourage counter-cyclical capital investments in economic downturns. Each slump, he reasoned, increased government's influence over the economy. The trend was toward state capitalism. In addition, he called for pegging wage increases to objective measures like profit, productivity, and inflation—this to drain the venom from labor-management relations. Objectively determined wage increases formed the kernel of what a *New York Times* editorial in the early 1980s termed "the best economic idea since Keynes." The idea came from a 1984 book by Martin L. Weitzman, an MIT economist, called *The Share Economy*. While his book has highly original emphases, Weitzman's ideas for industrial society closely track those of *Concept of the Corporation*.

Drucker's unambiguously pro-business proposals went unnoticed at GM. Marvin Coyle, head of Chevrolet, denounced the book as "an attack on the company, as hostile as anything ever mounted by the left." Alfred P. Sloan treated it "as if it did not exist." When Charles Wilson, GM's CEO, who'd been ill while Drucker was working on the book, mentioned that he was giving *Concept* to his friends as a Christmas present, Sloan cautioned, "I wouldn't do it, Mr. Wilson. Your friends might think you endorse Mr. Drucker's book." Years later Sloan confided to Drucker, "I had thought several times of writing my memoirs but always decided against it as being too self-important. But your book forced me to do the job. It made it clear to me that I had a duty to set the record straight." Any GM executive found reading *Concept of the Corporation* was quietly told, "Better go to work for Mr. Ford."[16]

In an exemplum of what *Concept* calls "the parochialism of the executive imagination," Chevrolet's Coyle was exercised by a letter Drucker had written to accompany his manuscript. Very tentatively, Drucker had broached the seditious idea that, to avoid anti-trust prosecutions in the postwar, GM should consider making a separate company out of Chevrolet. More offensive was Drucker's suggestion that GM consider changing its policies on, among other things, employee and customer relations. "I argued only that a policy, any policy, tends to outlive itself after twenty years and that the reconversion of the company to peacetime production . . . gave GM an exceptional opportunity for fresh thinking." Management didn't see it that way. One executive told him: "We have spent twenty years thinking through . . . these policies. . . . We *know* they are right. You might as well ask us to change the law of gravity." Management at GM, Drucker dryly remarks, was a branch of theology.[17]

Seen in the context of the times, GM had a compelling reason to deny its paternity of *Concept of the Corporation*. It was in the midst of a 113-day strike, losing millions daily, and in danger of losing the war for public opinion with the UAW. Drucker's other proposals were bad enough; his insistence that the corporation was "affected with the public interest" and should show "social responsibility" was insupportable. Reuther's key demand in the strike, after all, was for GM, which lost $2 billion in war contracts on V-J day, to raise wages 30 percent but, to show its concern for the *public interest* in low prices and low inflation, *not* raise prices. GM should "open its books," Reuther demanded, to show that it could afford to keep prices stable. Reuther's strategy was to place unions on the side of consumers, to use the strike to put an egalitarian stamp on the new society. GM could hardly align itself with a book echoing this incipient "socialism."

Drucker is somewhat disingenuous in depicting himself as *persona non grata* throughout GM. After all, Charles Wilson was in his corner. Persuaded by the worker-friendly logic of *Concept of the Corporation,* Wilson made Drucker his consultant on employee relations and established an employee relations staff, apart from labor relations. (Drucker later found out that Wilson wanted *him* to be GM's vice president for employee relations.) In 1947, as a first step toward the "responsible worker" and "the self-governing plant community," Wilson created a company-wide contest called "My Job and Why I Like It." Workers were asked to write candid essays on that theme. An astonishing 300,000 submitted essays, some running to 3,000 words. Even a sample of these essays showed that the workers had a strong "desire to identify themselves with product and company and to be held responsible for quality and performance," to quote Drucker's gloss of the findings. Many of them said they had ideas on how to improve their jobs, but nobody at GM had ever bothered to ask for them. Eager to follow up on this survey, Wilson moved to set up what he may have been the first to call "quality circles."[18]

"And then the whole program was hastily dropped," Drucker writes, and the results of the "My Job and Why I Like It" survey were suppressed. The UAW had threatened a company-wide strike if GM acted on the Wilson/Drucker plan. Wilson dispatched Drucker to talk to Walter Reuther. His outlook had changed since GM, which did not "open its books" but did increase its prices, had humbled the UAW in the strike the year before. He had trimmed his hopes and so had the union movement. Its commitment to fight on behalf of a broad progressive social agenda was weakening in the face of corporate resistance to union demands and conservative attacks. Labor was fast becoming an interest group fighting for nothing nobler than "more."[19]

Displaying the parochialism of the liberal-labor imagination, Reuther was blunt: "Managers should manage and workers work," he told Drucker, "and to demand of workers that they take responsibility for what is management's job imposes an intolerable burden on the working man." As Drucker noted, GM executives used this very argument against Wilson's work-improvement plan. Workers had no business adopting the managerial attitude toward their work: "*We are being paid for knowing how to organize work and job,*" they maintained, "*or at least for knowing it better than people with much less experience, much less education, and much lower income.*" In other words, "Managers should manage and workers work."

FOR ALL Drucker's conservative realism, *Concept of the Corporation* appealed to New Deal values at a time when the country was moving beyond the New Deal. With the war-heated economy running at full employment, with real wages up 27 percent since 1943, and, in what one historian calls "the most progressive redistribution of income in the twentieth century," with the family incomes of poorer Americans up 60 percent since Pearl Harbor, memories of the Depression were fading. The German economist Werner Sombart once proposed a memorable answer to the question: Why is there no socialism in America? Socialist egalitarianism, he wrote, foundered on "shoals of roast beef." Drucker's new industrial society foundered on the immense shoal of roast beef that was the postwar boom. America was about to experience what Edward Heath, the former British prime minister, called "the greatest prosperity the world had ever known."[20]

GM would flourish in the boom. Success would seem to vindicate the eternal verity of its policies. In time, however, its cars would become symbols of mass-produced, low-quality, made-in-America goods. (Visiting Los Angeles, import land, in the early 1990s, one GM designer reported, "Many people out there didn't even know Chevrolet still made cars.") The mood inside its plants was fatal to the quality consumers were demanding. GM treated its line employees with time-honored brutishness. "The combination of mindless, monotonous work, unrelenting regimentation, and inhumane supervision," the ULCA sociologist Ruth Milkman writes of a plant she studied for years, "made the workers feel like prisoners, and they routinely employ the metaphor of the plant as prison in discussing their jobs." GM employees accepting an early retirement buyout offer gave her some of their reasons for leaving:

> It was a hellhole working on the line for GM.
>
> I hated working for GM, the way they were running the plant.
>
> I was sick of working at GM. It's tedious, boring. The ladies' room was twenty-eight steps up, with no chairs, benches or stools. We used to sit on the sinks. And the GM bosses they treated us like a master does slaves.
>
> I was unhappy with the job; they were constantly jerking you around, turning you into a cog, putting you in worse jobs.

Even though they could get attractive discounts on the latest models, many of the men and women who worked at this Linden, New Jersey plant in the 1970s and early 1980s refused to buy GM cars. They drove Fords.

Only in the mid–1980s, with Japanese imports gaining a growing share of the U.S. market, with its products derided as cheap goods, with its usual method of motivation by fear no longer working on its younger workers—only *in extremis* would GM revive the Wilson/Drucker strategy of 1947. Belatedly it would try to improve "the quality of working life" by instituting quality circles, by training the "responsible worker," and by taking other Wilson/Drucker steps. "Whether this strategy will work, it is much too early to tell," Drucker wrote in 1993, a year after GM, with losses running at $365 million a week, ousted its management and brought in a new team. "But it will certainly produce a very different General Motors."[21]

The lyrics of *Concept of the Corporation* would spread beyond GM to the rest of corporate America. Assuming control of Ford in 1946, young Henry Ford II would rebuild his failing company on the GM decentralized template, acknowledging his debt to *Concept of the Corporation*. General Electric would also use the book (and Drucker as consultant) in its 1950 reorganization. And by the mid–1980s, as we have seen, Drucker had converted most of the *Fortune* 500 to decentralization. Still, *Concept's* music would be heard elsewhere.

"My popularity in Japan, where I am credited with substantial responsibility for the emergence of the country as a major economic power," Drucker wrote in a 1993 Epilogue to a new edition of *Concept of the Corporation*, "and for the performance and productivity of its industry, goes back to *Concept of the Corporation,* which was almost immediately translated into Japanese, eagerly read and applied." The Japanese heard the music.[22]

"People are a resource and not a cost. The Japanese have accepted that idea and we haven't," Drucker told Warren Bennis. Somehow a copy of the "My Job and Why I Like It" survey got to Toyota in the early 1950s, Drucker says, and became the basis for Toyota's efforts to instill the ethic of Drucker's "responsible worker" dedicated to quality work. Drucker's call for a guaranteed annual income became Japan's lifetime employment policy. In *Concept of the Corporation,* Drucker could find no solution to a besetting problem of the American workplace: With the ever-present threat of layoffs hanging over them, American workers were fools to show more of their abilities or to suggest efficiencies that could put themselves and their coworkers out of their jobs. Lifetime employment solved that problem for the Japanese. Assured of his job, a Toyota worker sought to *increase* efficiency; treating people as a resource was good for the bottom line. Through Drucker-influenced steps like these, postwar Japan transformed what had long been some of the world's worst labor-management relations into a model of the industrial society. For over thirty years, Drucker would visit Japan every two or three years to hold seminars for Japanese managers. These reinforced the message of *Concept of the Corporation* and succeeding books.[23]

Few policies last twenty years, Drucker, the champion of systematic abandonment and innovation, preaches. Lifetime employment in the major industries served Japan well for longer than that. Now, Drucker fears, Japan may have to abandon that policy under the pressure of the same world economy that is eroding our few social protections from the New Deal. "I hope that Japan (even in the radical industrial transformation we are now going through) will maintain the basic commitment to the mutuality of obligations between employer and employee, and to the employing organization as being a community of interest for all those who work there," Drucker said in a 1996 interview.[24]

Politically, it will be harder for the Japanese to break this social bond of promises and responsibilities than it has been for Americans to tear up the New Deal's federal safety net for poor children or than it *may* be to persuade Americans to take the security out of Social Security by hazarding part of the Social Security Trust Fund in the

stock market or to take the social out by privatizing individual accounts. American financial, corporate, and intellectual elites appear to
think that security is something America can no longer afford in
the competitive world economy, and these elites finance the politics
of the status quo and justify it in their public talk and purchased writing. Here is the downside of the postpolitical mood: elites dominate
while the public retreat in defensive cynicism from the squalid farces of
public life.

But tides turn. Mounting social pain may lead to calls for an international New Deal to regulate hours, wages, and working conditions,
to allow Third World workers to organize unions, and to protect the
global environment. Societies need some degree of shelter from the indifferent storms of a new world economy where American steel workers making $13 an hour must compete with Brazilian steel workers
making $1.28.[25]

Just how much protection societies can afford without losing
economic dynamism, was at the center of a principled debate between Drucker and his friend, and fellow Bennington teacher, the
Hungarian economic historian Karl Polanyi. While Polanyi was writing *The Great Transformation,* his study of the emergence of market
society, he would talk out his ideas in conversations with Drucker
through the Vermont nights. In his Author's Acknowledgments to
*The Great Transformation,* Polanyi thanked Peter and Doris Drucker.
"The latter and his wife were a source of sustained encouragement, notwithstanding their wholehearted disagreement with the
author's conclusions." On Drucker's account in *Adventures of a Bystander,* Polanyi passionately believed in a third way between capitalism and Marxian socialism—in a society, Drucker writes, "that
would provide at the same time economic growth *and* stability, freedom *and* equality." Drucker was willing to settle for much less, not the
good society but the "bearable society," which is why he gave *The*

*Future of Industrial Man* its subtitle, *A Conservative Approach,* and why Polanyi criticized the book as a "tepid compromise."[26]

From his researches into the human degradation of early English industrialism, Polanyi knew the damage that the unregulated market could inflict on society, community, and the family; so he was willing to err on the side of state intervention in the economy to protect society. Drucker, mindful of the necessity—for justice and social decency and not just for wealth—of a free economy, erred on the conservative side. The pursuit of the good society, he feared (with Soviet Communism no doubt on his mind) would end either in statist tyranny or economic collapse. In Drucker's bearable society "we would maintain freedom by paying a price: the disruption, the divisiveness, and the alienation of the market. . . . In such a society we would be less concerned with the greater good and more with the lesser evil."[27]

That is the price we continue to pay for the market. Until recently it had national borders, with winners and losers within each country. Now it is worldwide and, except for their elites, whole countries can be losers. Whether humankind will pay that price for American-proof economic freedom history will tell. But the issue is as Polanyi and Drucker framed it: a conflict between the goods of social security and economic growth.

# 5

# The Basic Disturbance
# of the Twentieth Century

THE BUSINESS of this chapter will be to discuss Drucker's
three nonmanagement books of the 1950s: *The New Society, America's
Next Twenty Years,* and *Landmarks of Tomorrow.* The variousness of the
subjects they deal with—from automation to religion, from demography to philosophy—resists summary generalization. What unites them
is Drucker's pragmatic faith in the future. "It does not minimize the
problems and challenges," Drucker writes of *Landmarks of Tomorrow*
(first published in 1959), in a 1995 Introduction to a new edition. "But
it looks at them as work to be done . . . rather than as burdens or
crises." Although mostly offstage in these books, the manager accounts
for a good deal of this attitude. Throughout the early 1950s Drucker
was working on his classic book, *The Practice of Management;* from 1949
when he left Bennington, he was teaching management at New York
University's graduate business school and consulting with the likes of
General Electric. The managerial outlook Drucker was assimilating
does not breathe the tragic sense of life. Problems are challenges. Organization planes down human weaknesses. Today creates tomorrow—it
doesn't just happen accidentally. This is a universe of provably vindi-
cated hope, and it was leaving its impress on Drucker, who had been so
doomy a decade before.

\* \* \*

HE HAD been warned: *Concept of the Corporation* was indeed regarded as something of a sport in economics and political science. "It dealt with a business—and yet it wasn't *economics*. It dealt with structure, organization, policy, constitutional principles, power relationships—yet it wasn't *government*." Reviewing the book for a professional journal, a leading political scientist wrote, "It is to be hoped that this promising young scholar will now devote his considerable talents to a more respectable subject."[1]

In fact, Drucker had found a subject he would *make* respectable. *Concept of the Corporation* gave his career a new trajectory. As we have seen, he began as a social scientist more interested in the social and political dimensions of large organizations like GM than in their economic purpose. By the late 1940s and early 1950s when *Concept of the Corporation* had propelled Drucker into management consulting, he evinces a new appreciation of the bottom line. The emphasis shifts from reforming the industrial corporation in the social and political directions marked out by *The End of Economic Man* and *The Future of Industrial Man* to a resigned acceptance of the unreconstructed corporation. The new tone sounds in a preface that Drucker wrote to a 1962 edition of *The New Society:*

> That there is no one easy answer to any real questions we now know and accept. We realize that there are facts to be faced and chores to be done. There are risks, difficulties and compromises. There are problems and opportunities. We are becoming non-utopian and anti-utopian, in the sharpest possible contrast to our parents and grandparents.
>
> *Concept of the Corporation* was as utopian as Peter Drucker would ever get.[2]

This evolved attitude towards business reflects a renewed sense of economic danger in the postwar world. It had taken the greatest war in history to end the Depression. "If war production should remain the only way out of a long-term depression," Drucker writes in *Concept of the Corporation,* "industrial society would be reduced to the choice between suicide through total war or suicide through total depression." It follows that a healthy economy helps prevent war and immunizes societies against the bacillus of fascism. Drucker's paramount goal now becomes making the industrial system *as it exists* work.

But in that system alienated work remains the norm—work that mocks human capacity. Moreover, world-competitive pressures on the system as it exists threaten such social integration as the corporation has achieved. Following Emile Durkheim, the French theorist of anomie, Drucker sees the industrial plant as the place where people uprooted by the pace of change can achieve a measure of social solidarity. If not "a haven in a heartless world," Marx's characterization of the family, the industrial plant is a source of stability and communal identity. This is the hope Drucker reposed in the giant corporation: The new society could be built around the integration achieved in the plant community. Time has ended that hope. In today's change-wracked workplace, beloved of faddist management gurus who don't have to work in one, social bonds can be difficult to forge and loyalty, whether up, down, or sideways, is hard to give. This is a poignant development for Drucker.[3]

*The New Society* stands midway in Drucker's shift from reform to critical pragmatism. *Time* magazine planned to put Drucker's likeness on the cover for a profile centered on *The New Society*. But North Korea suddenly invaded South Korea, and the cover went instead to that momentous event.[4]

DRUCKER SAW *The New Society* as distilling and systematizing the visions of *Industrial Man* and *Concept of the Corporation*. But it also breaks new conceptual ground—starting with the Introduction.[5]

In seventeen pages Drucker powerfully re-imagines "The Industrial World Revolution," the title of the Introduction. "The world revolution of our time is 'made in U.S.A.,'" the counterintuitive first sentence announces. That revolution is the system of mass production invented, in fateful 1914, by Henry Ford. The concepts undergirding his assembly-line system have since been applied outside the factory; mass production is *"a general principle for organizing people to work together."* From the Manhattan Project in World War II to the modern office, Ford's mass production is the grammar of work. In Aldous Huxley's *Brave New World,* the Alphas and Betas acknowledge Ford's place as the twentieth century's human engineer.

> Ford, we are twelve; oh make us one
> > Like drops within the social river.
> O make us now together run
> > As swiftly as thy shining flivver.[6]

Nearly everyone in the new society works together, in an organization, with others. This represents an historic change. "A hundred . . . years ago most people were still on the farm, tilling a few acres with no help other than from their families. Most craftsmen then worked for themselves, or with a hired man or two. . . . Except for soldiers, clergymen, and teachers—very small groups a century ago—hardly anyone worked for an institution." While most people could not *subsist* independently, they could *produce* independently. Fordism, which took the skill out of work, changed all that. Now people can be productive only through organizations structured, if only in attenuated form, along mass-production lines. Drucker is eloquent on one unanticipated consequence of this new dependency: "The picture of a man all by himself on the empty heath tending a high-speed lathe is perhaps the most screaming, bitter, satire on our civilization that could be imagined; it is

> ### The Managerial Viewpoint
>
> "What the worker needs is to see the plant as if he were a manager. Only thus can he see his part, from his part he can reach the whole. This 'seeing' is not a matter of information, training courses, conducted plant tours, or similar devices. What is needed is the actual experience of the whole in and through the individual's work."
>
> —*The New Society* (1950)

a picture of utter frustration, utter emptiness and complete damnation." The organization produces, not the individual.[7]

Under mass production, the "divorce of the worker from the product and the means of production" becomes "essential and absolute." For Marx, this state of alienation was transient, to be healed on the great day when the workers take over the means of production. But socialist mass production, it turns out, is no different in its effects on workers from capitalist mass production. It's the mass production that's revolutionary, not the socialism.[8]

Under mass production, unemployment becomes a social toxin and an existential terror. The worker cannot produce without the organization. So when the organization fails, the worker loses everything—the capacity to be productive along with status, function, and dignity—and he is easy prey for the libels of scapegoating extremists. That is why modern states cannot permit a wholesale failure of economic organizations. They cannot regard slumps, as nineteenth-century governments did, as acts of nature before which they are helpless. They must intervene either to prevent slumps through overall management of the economy or to hasten recovery from them. Given the trouble analysts have in pinning down the economic causes of the Depression, Drucker doubts the efficacy of prevention. "Economic policy must thus concentrate less on eliminating the economic causes of depressions, whatever they may be," he wrote in *Concept of the Corporation,* "than on overcoming the depression-caused inability to get going again." To end depressions governments must have new powers over economy and society, powers that infringe on economic freedom and can threaten individual liberty. But that can't be helped. Mass unemployment cannot be permitted. It brought forth fascism and war. It might do so again.[9]

The mass-production revolution of industrialism, Drucker writes, is the "basic disturbance" of the twentieth century. Communism and fascism were "reactions" to it. Communism outlawed unemployment. Fascism sought to transcend it, and the other problems of industrial order, through war, which also ended the Depression in the U.S. Drucker presciently warns of the dangers of an economy reliant on defense spending to sustain employment: "For if this country . . . were to make its defense program a function of its domestic employment situation," he wrote as early as 1945, "it would become impossible to conduct a constructive and well-thought out foreign policy or to develop any lasting international collaboration." Fifteen years later, President Dwight D. Eisenhower issued a similar warning about "the military-industrial complex." Drucker identified the danger before the complex had congealed.[10]

Now, Drucker continues, in the period of the Cold War, the U.S. must show the world a democratic alternative to totalitarianism and war. It must devise new institutions for the new economy of mass pro-

---

### The Proper Study of Mankind

"The literature on management organization is growing . . . especially in this country; and it seems to be increasingly dedicated to the proposition that *the proper study of mankind is organization.*"

—*The New Society* (1950)

duction, because, "If the model is not furnished by the West, if it is not a model of a free industrial society, the model will be that of a slave industrial society."[11]

THE REST of *The New Society* lays out the features of what Drucker's subtitle terms "The Anatomy of Industrial Order." First to be addressed is the "Industrial Enterprise," the new society's defining institution. The next five sections analyze the problems of industrial order raised by the enterprise—especially "the wage issue" between management and labor.[12]

Drucker borrows Marxian logic to make us see anew. "We still think and talk of the basic problems of an industrial society as problems that can be solved by changing the system, that is the superstructure of political organization. Yet the real problems lie within the enterprise." This is a fresh frame of thought (though Drucker's Marx-like subordination of politics has a determinist ring to it). Like fascism and communism, many of the problems of the new society are reactions to the basic disturbance of mass production.[13] Drucker is saying: Get work right and social problems will right themselves. The enterprise is our "representative institution," "a mirror in which we look when we want to see ourselves." Unless we like what we see, unless the enterprise reflects our basic beliefs, "industrial society cannot survive." Drucker lapses here into the argument by apocalypse of his first two books.[14]

What do we see, then, in looking at the industrial enterprise? We see a new social order. A small group of people at the top command the enterprise. The civilian equivalent of kings and generals, they are familiar from history. A large number of people perform the day-to-day work of the enterprise. We certainly recognize them: they are yesterday's farmers and servants. (Drucker's 1994 *Atlantic Monthly* essay points out that farmers and domestic servants were the two largest groups in the workforce as late as 1900.) In the middle of the social order of the enterprise is a large expanding group of technicians, managers, and professionals. Less than 10 percent of the U.S. workforce in 1880, they total 30 percent in the 1990s. They are the industrial middle class. They are what's new about the new society.[15]

In the enterprise as microcosm the employee is an industrial citizen just as he is a citizen in the macrocosm of the state. *Concept of the Corporation* expanded on the notional rights of industrial citizenship. *The New Society* begins with its obligations. "For the proper functioning in the industrial enterprise," Drucker writes, "its members, down to the last sweeper and wheelbarrow-pusher, must have a 'managerial attitude' toward their own work and toward the enterprise; they must look upon it as their own and upon themselves as 'citizens' rather than as 'subjects.'" The managerial attitude is an "attitude which makes the individual see his job, his work and his product the way the manager sees them . . ." The productivity of the enterprise depends on all employees adopting it, since, "The major incentives to productivity and efficiency are social and moral rather than financial."[16]

This is among the most controversial passages in Drucker's work. Drucker sees the problem of the worker's alienation as, in the first instance, a psychological problem. To raise employee productivity, the enterprise can dispense with the carrot (higher wages) and the stick (the threat of being fired). It is enough to implant the "managerial attitude" in the employee's psyche. Thus programmed, the employee endures the alienation and spirit-cracking boredom of industrial work as serving a higher managerial end. He also learns to live with the inherent instability of employment in an enterprise answerable to the market. This is industrial citizenship on management's terms. Work remains alienated. The market still rules. Nothing has changed except the attitude of the worker.

In a recent article on an Ohio manufacturing company, the *New*

*York Times* quoted its union-busting CEO, who had been sending more and more of the company's work to installations in the non-union South, revealing the manipulative face of the managerial attitude. "Unionism is going down," he said, "because corporations have changed their views. We empower our people now. They work in teams with shared responsibilities. It's not management versus labor in the plants now. We're all one for the shareholder." Certainly he was all for the shareholder, being one himself—and with every layoff or cut in worker pay his shares grew in value.[17]

In fairness, Peter Drucker rejects manipulation of this or any other kind. He employs a phrase "manipulative paternalism," that describes what that Ohio manufacturer is up to. He even detects overtones of manipulation in profit-sharing plans, since they bind a worker to an employer, inhibiting the worker's exercise of his economic freedom— "Every worker needs to escape the wrong job." In *Management: Tasks, Responsibilities, Practices* (1974) he writes:

> An employer has no business with a man's personality. Employment is a specific contract calling for specific performance . . . Any attempt to go beyond this is usurpation. It is immoral as well as an illegal intrusion of privacy. It is abuse of power. An employee owes no "loyalty," he owes no "love" and no "attitudes"—he owes performance and nothing else.

Yet, writing in 1950, he sees "the managerial attitude" as non-manipulative; indeed as "in harmony with the demand that the individual achieve the 'dignity of the person' in which a Western society believes."[18]

Drucker is searching for a way to reconcile the dignity of the person with the coercive element in work. He wants even the meanest worker, "the last sweeper and wheel-barrow pusher," to take pride in his work, not for management's sake but for his own integrity of personality. If work is nothing more than a drudgery of outward compli-

**The "six common mistakes" made in designing managerial jobs.**

1. Since any managerial job is likely to be "terminal," it must be big enough to keep the manager challenged. Designing jobs that are too small is an invitation for the manager to "retire on the job."

2. Worse than the job that's too small is the job that is not really a job. That would be an "assistant to" job. That job can "corrupt" the organization by turning decent people into toadies and wire-pullers. "This does not mean that the title 'assistant' has to be eschewed—the reality should be avoided."

3. Managing is not "full-time work." The manager needs something to do when he's not managing. As well as manager, he should be a career professional with work in his field to keep him from "trying to do his subordinates' work."

4. "It is a mistake to design a job so that it requires continuous meetings, continuous 'cooperation and coordination.' " The job should be such that it can be done by one person and the people he manages. And if one cannot meet and work, one cannot travel and work, either.

5. Titles should not be used in lieu of a raise—or in lieu of a job. The proliferation of empty titles—the purchasing clerk dignified into the Coordinator of Materials Planning—creates dissatisfaction among those whose titles are not upgraded. "The rule should be: for first-rate work we pay— and pay well. But we change title only when a man's function, position, and responsibility change."

6. Jobs should not be "widow makers." The term originated in the days of the clipper ships, when it was used to describe ships that "tended to get out of control and kill people." Some jobs are like that. The rule is: "If a job has defeated, in a row, two men who in their previous assignments have done well, it should be restructured."

—*Management: Tasks, Responsibilities, Practices* (1973)

ance achieved at the price of inward rage, self-disgust, and resentment, as it apparently was for the GM workers heard from in Chapter 4, then the workplace is truly a hell of alienation with nothing but bad social and political consequences beyond the factory gates or office doors. Drucker refuses to accept any state of things in which work like this is the norm. He holds out instead an ideal that is poorly conveyed in the "managerial attitude": the ideal of the "responsible worker." Asked recently to define "responsibility," he writes:

> Responsibility is both external and internal. Externally it implies accountability to some person or body and accountability for specific performance. Internally it implies commitment—if I sound like a very old schoolmaster, that's what I am—and these are Aristotelian terms (and Plato's too) clarified and defined by (a) Thomas Aquinas and (b) by The Federalist Papers (largely following Montesquieu, by the way). The Responsible Worker is not only a worker who is accountable for specific results but also who has authority to do whatever is necessary to produce these results and who, finally, is committed to these results as a *personal* achievement.

This is fine as far as it goes; workers of every description ought to feel this way about their work, and there would be less worker alienation if they did. But one can easily imagine that Ohio manufacturer saying, "That's exactly what I mean by 'empowerment.' " (Drucker: "I hate the word empowerment and have never used it nor ever will.") Empowerment in his company means unprotected by a union, means no security of employment beyond the day's work, means constant pressure to perform lest the company move South or to Mexico or some other locale with no unions and workers made pliant by need.

A worker can be responsible in Drucker's admirable sense only if power and fear are kept out of the picture. Drucker that can happen if the power the employer has over the worker is legitimate, in which case it becomes authority, power made right by the worker's consent to its rightness. But even legitimate power, as the authors of the Federalist Papers insisted, is likely to be abused unless it is checked by other and equal power. In the industrial society the worker should be able to withhold his labor if the employer abuses his power. He can do that without fear of losing his job, however, only with a union in back of him; that neutralizes the power element and its penumbra of fear to the point where you can begin to talk about the responsible worker.

Drucker's similitude of enterprise to polity and worker to citizen is less problematic than his call for the managerial attitude; it is just misleading. Industrial citizenship is out the window if the enterprise cannot perform. Even "Archangels in command of an industrial enterprise would have to make profitability as much the first law of their actions as the 'greediest capitalist.'" Here Drucker's analogy breaks down. You won't lose your U.S. citizenship if the country fails to show a profit. But the industrial citizen can lose his industrial citizenship under these circumstances. The asymmetry of power between the enterprise and the worker, however, is as nothing next to the power the market wields over both—the best, union-accepting, employer, the most responsible worker. The market knows no citizens and respects no values. Drucker's industrial citizen is the subject of a tornado.[19]

"IS WAGE," Drucker asks, "to be considered primarily a current cost incurred in payment for a commodity consumed in the production process? Or is it primarily a future cost of conserving and increasing the human resources of production?"[20]

Reasonably enough, both. To the enterprise wages are costs; to the worker, income. Writing when, "It would be a rare day without a wage conflict in the headlines," Drucker seeks industrial comity through a wage formula at once "enterprise-oriented" and "worker-oriented." For the enterprise, the focus on wage rate per hour has left it with an inflexible wage burden that only goes up. ("Our wages have become frozen at the high point.") The enterprise needs wages, instead, to rise or fall with prices, productivity, and inflation. No union could accept flexible wages unless the new formula offered workers something big in return. As we have seen, it does: security of employment, a commitment by the enterprise to guarantee the worker an annual income, a percentage of his full-time salary, whether he works or, in the troughs of the business cycle, is put out of work. There is a trade-off: wage flexibility for income security. (Later, Drucker adds the fine print: the worker must *repay* the money given him while he was laid off once he gets back to work.)[21]

Drucker's basic formula satisfies key demands on both sides. More, it takes the accelerator off the wage-price spiral that we saw surface in the GM negotiations with the UAW in 1946. Ever-increasing wages and ever-increasing prices are a recipe for inflation. There is a vital public interest, therefore, in settling the wage issue on a new basis.

There cannot have been many better ideas in the economic air in 1950. The Drucker formula *is* "the best idea since Keynes." Think of the billions in lost income our wage-centered labor management relations have cost striking or laid-off workers. Think of the billions in research and development, in reinvestment and capital investment, lost by American corporations since 1950. Finally think of the cruel costs of wage-price-led inflation: for those on fixed incomes, a fall in the standard of living; for government, seas of red ink and cutbacks in public investment and public services vital to tomorrow's productivity. Think of the ghost towns of the upper midwest in the postwar recessions, the only means left to government to stop inflation, the blasted dreams, the broken families, the shattered communities. With tragic clairvoyance Drucker saw where the wage issue was heading.

Having projected an alternative future for postwar capitalism Drucker turns to another snag on the road to the industrial society— the nearly universal hostility to profit. Partly, this stems from a public ignorance about profit that Drucker has spent decades trying to dispel. "[T]he essential fact about profit is that there is no such thing," he wrote in the *Wall Street Journal* in 1973. "There are only costs . . . costs of doing business and costs of staying in business; costs of labor and raw materials, and costs of capital; costs of today's jobs and tomorrow's pensions." Drucker is right that business leaders rarely make this case for "profit," but then they may not want to draw attention to their personal share of it.

More than misunderstanding accounts for the hostility to profit; there is also resentment about exorbitant executive salaries, which is "not economic at all but social—they are felt to be a denial of justice and fairness." Drucker wrote those words in 1950; in 1997 he told *Forbes:* "Few top executives can even imagine the hatred, contempt, and even fury that has been created—not primarily among blue-collar workers who never had an exalted opinion of the 'bosses'—but among their middle management and professional people." Though he is strongly against them, Drucker understands the logic of high executive salaries—among other mitigations, the tiers of management in the enterprise mandate increasingly sharp differentials in salary. But workers do not accept such rationales, and they won't be talked into accepting them. "The mere mention of the 'fat' salaries of the bosses," he notes, "is the one thing that never fails to arouse emotion in a union meeting. . . ."[22]

The salaries are toxic: "The resentment against the big salaries of the top executives poisons the political and social relations within the plant, aggravates the difficulty of communication between management and employees, and reduces management's chance to be accepted as the government of the plant." And the salaries are hell on the managerial outlook.[23]

Capitalism gets its reputation for greed primarily from executive salaries, which have only grown more outrageous since 1950. "Since 1980," John Sweeney, the president of the AFL–CIO, writes, "while workers' real wages have fallen, total CEO pay rose by 499 percent. Back in 1960, the average CEO earned forty-one times more than the average workers. By 1995, the average CEO raked in 145 times more than the average worker." A *Business Week* survey found that executive salaries for 1996 were *209 times* the pay of the average worker. Drucker needs no tutelage on a trend he has decried for fifty years. Citing J. P. Morgan, "who certainly cannot be accused of not liking money," on the evils of big salaries, Drucker, circa 1996, says that the ratio of pay between worker and executive can be no higher than twenty to one without injury to company morale. On Drucker's recommendation, his friend, Max De Pree, chairman of Herman Miller, a *Fortune* 500 Michigan furniture maker, adopted the twenty-to-one ratio, tying executive raises to the overall performance of the company. "People have to think about the common good," De Pree told the *Wall Street Journal*. Executives to whom that sentiment is foreign are bad enough; those who downsize their companies to enhance the value of corporate stocks, including that portion of their compensation derived from stocks, earn Drucker's special scorn:[24]

> "What is new," he recently told *Wired*, "and by no means desirable is the way in which these layoffs are being carried out. This is what bothers me. A lot of top managers enjoy cruelty. There is no doubt that we are in a period in which you are a hero if you are cruel. In addition, what's absolutely unforgivable is the financial benefit top management people get for laying off people. There is no excuse for it. No justification. This is morally and socially unforgivable, and we will pay a heavy price for it."[25]

"An industrial system can function and survive only on a profit margin adequate to the demands of the future," Drucker wrote in 1950. "The adequacy, if not the existence of the profit margin is seriously threatened by the worker's rejection of profitability." And the workers reject profits because they see them going abroad to create new factories, to stockholders in dividends, to piratical salaries, and not into job retraining or raises or improved working conditions.

Evidence from the nineties suggests that workers have more grounds than they did in 1950 for their prejudice against profits. The surge in profitability recorded in the mid-90s was not the result of increasing productivity, which grew by only 1 percent each year in the 1980s and 1990s. It "mainly reflects," the economist Lawrence Mishel writes in *The American Prospect,* "business success in restraining wage growth. If the return to capital—profits and interest income per dollar of assets—in 1994 and 1995 (10.66 percent) had been instead at the average of the cyclical peaks during the 1959–1979 period (8.37 percent), then hourly compensation would have been 3.6 percent higher. . . . A 3.6 percent wage loss might not sound like much, until you realize that the entire growth in hourly compensation over the 1989–1996 period has been just 2.8 percent. In other words," Mishel concludes, confirming the suspicion common among American workers that profits are coming out of their incomes, "had this shift in income from labor to capital not occurred, recent wage growth would have been more than double its actual rate."[26]

*The New Society* pulls in threads left dangling by its predecessors. For example, the question of how to wring social meaning out of making can openers or lamp shades. The can opener *is* meaningful to the manager. His bonus depends on how many sell, and he knows the complex business plan into which the can opener fits. So, the only answer Drucker can see to the meaning problem is the widespread adoption of the manager's attitude. As an example of its consolations, Drucker holds up a baler he saw at GM, who got meaning out of his dirty work (baling scrap metal) by imagining how each individual scrap of metal went to make up a part and how the parts fitted into the finished cars. This vision of the whole is his managerial *frisson.* Of course his musings bear no relation to how the cars really get made; nevertheless, they keep him happy in his work. Drucker's baler does not inhabit the same world, though he works for the same company, as the men and women Ruth Milkman interviewed in New Jersey.[27]

Still, even these hard cases might attain the managerial perspective if they were part of management, sharing in its decisions and profits and being willing to sacrifice from their wages to cover its losses. That was Walter Reuther's hope in his "open-the-books" strike against GM—before he lowered his sights to "Managers should manage, workers work." He wanted the people with the largest stake in the success of GM, workers with families to feed, to participate in its management decisions—to represent, for example, the consumer by speaking out against unjustified price increases. Alfred P. Sloan abominated that idea. Peter Drucker merely dismisses it. "There can be no participation of the worker in the management of the business," he writes in *Concept of the Corporation,* "which, in the worker's own interest, must be in the hands of trained executives working for the business, and not for the union or for the government."[28]

Usually unpersuaded by narrowly economic arguments, Drucker sounds like an accountant here. Yes, economic democracy would entail inefficiency, notably in decision-making. But Drucker has long argued that Japanese businesses have not been hampered by the glacial pace at which they make decisions. More important, workers participating in management would have a managerial attitude that grew out of managerial experience, not a simulacrum sham cooked up by the personnel department. Surely that would be worth a great deal.

Finally, we come to the "self-governing plant community" and what a disappointment *it* turns out to be. Drucker's "self-governing plant community" means worker control—but of the cafeteria, the blood bank, and the annual summer picnic. This sounds harmless enough until you remember that the self-governing plant community was one of Drucker's answers to the worker's demands for status, function, and equal opportunity in the postwar era. Drucker cannot bring himself to accept worker participation in management or in the pace and design of work: that would be too much intervention in the economic dynamics *à la* Karl Polanyi. Yet he is intellectually honest and compassionate enough to see the real problems—was, indeed, the first to see them. So, as a gesture toward their solution, he comes up with the managerial attitude, and the near beer of the self-governing plant community. In *Industrial Man* Drucker dug himself into a diagnostic hole by depicting the problems of industrialism in an end-of-days-light. The self-governing plant community would not look so thread-bare if it were meant to improve morale or to achieve other equally modest aims.

THE LEAST *written* of Drucker's books, *America's Next Twenty Years* (1957) reads like a course of printed lectures, with a "that-settles-that" clap of the hands at the end of each of its six dash-length chapters.

In a highly favorable review in the *New York Times Book Review* the economist Robert L. Heilbroner compactly defined Drucker's approach to the future: "His premise is that the forces destined to shape our future economic environment are already here at hand, and it remains therefore only to scrutinize the present in order to foretell the future. As Mr. Drucker says, 'The major events that determine the future have already happened—irrevocably.' "[29]

Of these events demographic change is the most reverberant. The Baby Boom has created a paradoxical new economic demography: "there are going to be more people, and hence more jobs, but not more people to fill the jobs." This is so because so many Baby Boomers will be in college, not in the labor force. How can we (in 1957) assume the Boomers will flock to college? Drucker predicts a surge in their numbers on the basis of another event that had already happened: the democratization of higher education. "It had long been clear," he writes, "that the mid-fifties would show whether there had been any real change in the educational habits of the country, or whether the GI Bill had just created a temporary bulge in college enrollment." Had the country been returning to the standard of 1940, a decline of as much as 30 percent in college enrollment could have been expected after the last GIs graduated. Instead, enrollment increased. The country's educational habits *had* changed. From the unexpected increases in the post-GI freshman classes of the mid-1950s, Drucker predicts the college explosion of the 1960s, and its result, announced in his chapter title, "The Coming Labor Shortage."[30]

Too many jobs chasing too few working-age people: this was not a recipe for a new depression. "The basic problem of economic policy in the two decades ahead should . . . not be unemployment but inflation." Heilbroner was "intrigued rather than fully persuaded" by Drucker's argument that inflation would arise from a labor shortage that bid up wages and prices. But, once again, the future bore Drucker out, if not on the causes of inflation in the 1970s, then on the fact of it. Twenty years later, as the economy grazed double-digit inflation, President Gerald Ford would pass out buttons marked WIN, "Whip Inflation Now," in the war against the new enemy. Drucker had seen this wage-price-led inflationary spiral coming since 1945. He had advocated a better way that could not only have prevented the pain of inflation, but the suffering of its cure, the government-induced recession of 1981–1982, the worst since the Great Depression.[31]

Drucker next turns to "The Promise of Automation," which is nothing less than "the human use of human beings," in the beckoning phrasing of Norbert Wiener, the father of cybernetics. Because of its pertinency to our time, the thinking behind Drucker's generally benign view of automation is worth exploring.[32]

"Automation is the technological revolution of the second half of the twentieth century," Drucker writes, "just as mass production was of the first half." Drucker sees automation as a system of seeing and planning and organizing work with or without machines. But, narrowly construed, automation is "the use of machines to run machines."

Decades before the personal computer, Drucker concedes "a sharp cut in employment for routine office work" and "dislocation unemployment" as people whose jobs were automated shift to new jobs, many of them in small businesses. Nevertheless, in the aggregate, even for the displaced workers who would now have a chance to do human work, "Socially, the shift in job opportunities . . . should be healthy." With his predictably constant candor, Drucker adds: "But it will still impose on management a responsibility to plan systematically for the retraining and placement of workers during the shift to automation."[33]

Drucker may have been right about his period, 1957–1977. From the perspective of the 1990s, however, when automation has gone digital in the "information revolution," any forecast of a socially "healthy" outcome from automation looks prematurely optimistic.[34]

A 1986 review of the research on job loss to technology carefully concludes: "Process and plant level investigations generally seem to point to significant displacement of labour. On the other hand, national level simulations more often reach the conclusion that there is no significant employment problem on hand." But if technology is not, (or not yet) judged on a country-wide basis, costing jobs, "yet the process of historical transition toward an informational society and a global economy is characterized by the widespread deterioration of living and working conditions for labor." These include: "declining, real wages, increasing inequality, and job instability in the United States; underemployment and stepped-up segmentation of the labor force in Japan . . ."

Furthermore, although the potential of information technologies could have provided for higher productivity, higher living standards, and higher employment simultaneously, once certain technological choices are in place, technological trajectories are "locked in," and the informational society could become at the same time (without the technological or historical necessity to be so) a dual society. . . .

The prevailing model for labor in the new, information-based economy is that of a *core labor force,* formed by information-based managers and by those whom [Robert] Reich calls "symbolic analysts," and a *disposable labor force* that can be automated and/or hired/fired, offshored, depending on market demand and labor costs.[35]

Heilbroner's lone criticism of *America's Next Twenty Years* was that Drucker treated automation "in a highly simplistic manner, which in avoiding the complexity of . . . issues skirts their full difficulty." Heilbroner's criticism applies to much of Drucker's work while somehow missing its point. Drucker's gift is to create concepts that light up problems and possibilities; others, by his light, can see the new solutions.[36]

*America's Next Twenty Years* is interesting as a catalogue of Drucker's prescience—right on inflation, right on America's growing reliance on imported raw materials, right on the college boom of the 1960's, right on the decline of union power, and right for this presentiment: "We must conclude this book on America's domestic future in the recognition that events beyond this country's borders may play, whether we like it or not, the determining role." For the biographer of Drucker's thought, *America's Next Twenty Years* is also noteworthy for exposing some of Drucker's assumptions—the givens of his thinking. The book's thinness, 114 pages, helps one see what one might miss on a crowded canvas.[37]

For example, in discussing productivity Drucker writes that the higher the capital investment per worker, "the higher the productivity—and, incidentally, the wages and salaries paid." Note the assumption here: better wages and salaries *will* follow increased productivity. Yet real wages declined by 12 percent between 1979 and 1994 while productivity rose by 24 percent; contra Drucker, higher productivity led not to higher wages, but to higher corporate profits, which have gone up by a whopping 499 percent since 1980, and to executive salaries beyond the dreams of avarice. Strictly speaking, wages are not a direct result of productivity; higher productivity only makes higher wages *possible*. Higher wages are a result either of the historic struggle and current balance of power between labor and management or a reflection, for those without union protection, of what the market will bear. And if the market is the world, wages, especially the wages of the less lucky, and the casualties of schools that focus on problems not on strengths, will increasingly be pegged to an ever-lower standard. "Those with third-world skills will earn third-world wages," Lester Thurow says, adding, "anything can be made anywhere on the face of the earth and sold everywhere else on the face of the earth."[38]

Another example: Writing of colleges that may outgrow their communal capacities, Drucker says, "If instead of growing themselves these giants were to help some smaller affiliated institutions in their area to grow, everybody might gain." The "affiliated" admittedly muddies the waters. Still, note the assumption: big institutions can act generously or at least according to enlightened self-interest. Depending on the context, this may or may not be true. The point is Drucker all but *expects* it to be true.[39]

Last example: In scanning "The Coming Issues in American Politics," Drucker focuses on racial progress.

We can expect the status of the Negro minority, during the next two decades, to change fairly drastically. Twenty years hence, the rapid industrialization of the South—combined with the continuous emigration of Negroes from the South—should mean that the traditional Southern pattern of rural and small-town segregation, except for a few isolated areas, will be a thing of the past.[40]

Here the assumption is that "industrialization" will change the segregated South. That leaves out the Supreme Court's historic reinterpretation of the Constitution, it leaves out the civil rights movement and its grassroots politics of protest, and it leaves out the Civil Rights Acts and their energetic enforcement by the Johnson Administration. These political forces ended the Jim Crow South, not industrialization and out-migration. Although President Eisenhower had sent troops to integrate a Little Rock high school while Drucker was at work on his book, he cannot see popular politics and government as agents of the greatest social change of the century.

Implicitly Drucker tends toward a kind of social/economic determinism. Mass production, not revolutionary politics, is "the basic disturbance of the twentieth century." Segregation will fall as a result of "industrialization." The "basic problems" of the industrial society cannot be solved by "the superstructure of political organization"; they stem from what Marx called "the social relations of production" and Drucker calls the social organization of the enterprise. In his *Atlantic Monthly* essay, Drucker writes: "if this century proves one thing, it is the futility of politics." Change has not come from political action, whether revolution or reform, but from social and economic forces working their way "like ocean currents below the hurricane-tormented surface of the sea."[41]

In a gloss on Drucker's "otherwise brilliant" *Atlantic* essay, E. J. Dionne, Jr., in his recent book calling for a progressive revival, *They Only Look Dead* (1996), takes on Drucker's "futility of politics."

The twentieth century turned out for the better in significant part because ordinary people were able to use politics in free societies to do extraordinary things—first to organize themselves and then to demand and win improvements in their living standards, create opportunities for their children and insist on basic social equality that is the essence of democracy as a way of life. This century, far from proving the futility of politics, is a history of the triumph of *democratic politics*.

Drucker's populist vision of twentieth-century history at the end of Chapter 2 of "ordinary people running the everyday concerns of business and institutions" as the real makers of history, needs Dionne's vision to complete it. Through this century of horrors, ordinary people could keep civilization going because democratic politics not only preserved but expanded their freedom.[42]

THE ORGANIZATION of *Landmarks of Tomorrow: A Report on the "Post-Modern" World* (1959) offers a good example of Drucker's refusal to construct book-length arguments that try to answer every objection and anticipate every question.

## CONTENTS

About all these chapters have in common is a sometimes wavering focus on what Drucker's original title called *The Future that Has Already Happened.* Each topic stands on its own bottom in Drucker's essay-as-chapter structure. "I have not even tried to pull together into one order of values and perceptions," he writes in the Introduction, "what are still individual pieces."[43]

*Landmarks of Tomorrow* is valuable in giving perhaps the fullest picture extant of Drucker's attitude toward the Cold War. He is clear that, "Communism is evil. Its driving forces are the deadly sins of envy and hatred." But what worries him more than Soviet Communism is runaway military technology that can destroy humanity. In an evocative passage he captures nuclear dread: "And who among us today has not had the shock of *knowing,* if only in a nightmare, the moment of fiery cloud and deadly rain, the irreversible moment when a power-drunk dictator, a trigger-happy colonel, or a simple misreading of a 'blip' on a radar screen will make us destroy ourselves?" He decries "the militarization of thinking," the coarsening of feeling, the Cold War has spawned. Propaganda seems to him a kind of deviltry. "Through systematic terror, through indoctrination, through systematic manipulation of stimulus, reward, and punishment, we can today break man and convert him into brute animal." Drucker wants this insidious capacity to wreak moral destruction denied to governments—and here again, his first-hand knowledge of fascism indicates the potential reach of the danger. He links the crisis in legitimacy faced by modern government to its possession of the powers to blow up the world and to capture the psyche through propaganda and group-think. "The first step toward survival is therefore to make government legitimate again by attempting to deprive it of these powers . . . by international action to ban such powers."[44]

There is an originality to Drucker's political-social outlook that continually surprises the student of his work. Thus in *The New Society* he comes out strongly against the Cold Warriors in the labor movement who would deny union membership to Communists: "The union must not be allowed to deprive minority groups of their citizenship rights as long as the law guarantees them these rights." To defend the rights of members of the Communist Party in 1950 took courage. In the same book he is strongly critical of the antiunion Taft–Hartley Act: "That the government's power under the Taft–Hartley Act to stop a strike by injunction so clearly strengthens the hand of the employer—even though it is to be used only when a strike threatens the national health, welfare, or safety—is a grave blemish and explains much of union resistance to the Act." While taking the ACLU position on the rights of dissenters and the liberal-labor position on Taft–Hartley, Drucker also criticizes businessmen for rarely venturing to defend profit in public—profit being a social necessity in Drucker's eyes, not the money-lust of the liberal imagination. Neither a liberal Liberal nor a conservative Conservative, through the decades Drucker has managed to keep his political balance while all around him America's intellectuals, falling left and right, were losing theirs.[45]

★    ★    ★

"AT SOME unmarked point during the last twenty years we imperceptibly moved out of the Modern Age and into a new, as yet nameless, era." *Landmarks of Tomorrow*'s first sentence *stipulates* an intriguing development. Characteristically, Drucker does not plumb its roots. Nor, forswearing any designs upon the future, does he review its likely consequences. "As I saw the job," he writes, "it was to understand rather than to innovate, to describe rather than to imagine." This he takes as the proper work of a "social ecologist," a participant-observer of the human habitat—social, economic, cultural.[46]

The first landmark of tomorrow is the displacement of the seventeenth-century mechanically-based Cartesian world view by a twentieth-century biologically-based world view. This is the change from cause to configuration mentioned earlier. Increasingly scientists deal with "configuration terms" like "Gestalt," "immunity," "metabolism," "syndrome," and "ecology." "Postmodern" is itself a configuration term. So, for that matter, is "management."[47]

This shift in metaphors is very far along now. The "Information Age" is modeled on human biology, not mechanics. Long before the

---

**The Drucker Test for "Organizational Dropsy"**

An organization is "sick"
—when promotion becomes more important to its people than accomplishment of their job
—when it is more concerned with avoiding mistakes than with taking risks
—and with counteracting the weaknesses of its members than with building on their strength
—and when good human relations become more important than performance and achievement.

"The moment people talk of 'implementing' instead of 'doing,' and of 'finalizing' instead of 'finishing,' the organization is already running a fever."

—*Landmarks of Tomorrow* (1959)

computer revolution Drucker saw the need for a new paradigm to fit the new technology. "We live in an age of transitions," he writes, capturing the inchoate shift in world view in one sentence, "an age of overlap, in which the old 'modern' of yesterday no longer acts effectively but still provides means of expression, standards of expectation, and tools of ordering, while the new 'post-modern' still lacks definition, expression, and tools, but effectively controls our actions and their impact."

Drucker's second landmark is the "new perception of order" encapsulated in the shift he traces from progress to innovation. The idea of progress cannot survive twentieth-century history. It was always a kind of metaphysical impertinence: history was in the saddle—man walked. Innovation, by contrast, is people-generated, purposeful, organized, but inherently risky change. "We no longer even understand the question whether change is by itself good or bad," Drucker writes. "We start out with the axiom that it is the norm. We do not see change as altering the order . . . We see change as being order in itself—indeed the only order we can comprehend today is a dynamic, a moving, a changing one." Drucker's celebration of innovation, the freedom to act anew, is incongruous with the economic and social determinism, those deep currents that rule beneath the storm-tormented sea, lodged in his assumptions.[48]

---

### Between the Ultras

"In the political, the social, the economic, even the cultural sphere, the revolutions of our time have been revolutions 'against' rather than revolutions 'for'. . . . On the whole throughout this period the man—or party—that stood for doing the positive has usually cut a pathetic figure; well-meaning but ineffectual, civilized but unrealistic, he was suspect alike to the ultras of destruction and the ultras of preservation and restoration."

—*Landmarks of Tomorrow* (1959)

The large organization is another landmark of the future. Thinking of the nonprofit organization as well as big business, Drucker writes: "The new organization is transforming work that was previously confined to individual effort. It does not replace the individual by organization; it makes the individual effective in teamwork." He worries most about the situation of the professional-as-employee, which more and more professionals (engineers, scientists, accountants, lawyers) will become in the era of the big organization. "Will he, though employed, be a citizen thinking of the common good and working for it? Or will he see only his dependence, follow narrowly his self-interest, and live by the creed that 'what is good for quality-control engineers is good for society?' "[49]

Drucker's fourth landmark of the future is education. The United States is in the midst of "an education explosion." No society before ours could afford to have more than a few educated people; "for throughout the ages to be educated meant to be unproductive." After all, Drucker notes, in his Great Cham of All Knowledge voice, "our word 'school'—and its equivalent in all European languages—derives from a Greek word meaning 'leisure.' "[50]

Making educated people productive is first among the challenges

---

### Learning by Doing

"The arts alone give direct access to experience. To eliminate them from education—or, worse, to tolerate them as cultural ornaments—is anti-educational obscurantism. It was foisted on us by the pedants and snobs of Hellenistic Greece who considered artistic performance fit only for slaves. . . .

"In book subjects a student can only do a student's work. All that can be measured is how well he learns, rather than how well he performs. All he can show is promise."

—*Landmarks of Tomorrow* (1959)

of our age—a challenge Drucker revisits forty years on, in *Post-Capitalist Society*. The role of the managed organization is to accomplish that task. Making educated people content is another matter: "Tomorrow everybody—or practically everybody—will have had the education of the upper class of yesterday, and will expect equivalent opportunities." However, only a "small minority" of the educated will be able to get ahead in the money sense. "That is why we face the problem of making every kind of job meaningful and capable of satisfying every educated man." A tall order when set against the intractable banality of making lamp shades and light bulbs.[51]

Drucker ends *Landmarks of Tomorrow* with the most nakedly religious sentiment yet expressed in his work: "The individual needs the return to spiritual values, for he can survive in the present human situation only by reaffirming that man is not just a biological and psychological being but also a spiritual being, that is creature, and existing for the purposes of his Creator and subject to Him."[52]

Where did He come from? Drucker found Him in a book by Sören Kierkegaard. Drucker was raised in a Lutheranism "so 'liberal' that it consisted of little more than a tree at Christmas and Bach cantatas at Easter." Then, while working in the Hamburg export firm as a young man, he came across Kierkegaard's *Fear and Trembling*. "I knew immediately that something had happened." Years later he wrote what he regards as his finest essay, on "The Unfashionable Kierkegaard."[53]

The nineteenth century, believing in progress, saw death as a terrible inconvenience. "It tried to get around death by organizing away its consequences," Drucker writes in a passage that unites the spiritual with the commercial in unexpected measures. "Life insurance is perhaps the most significant institution of nineteenth-century metaphysics; its proposition to 'spread the risks' shows most clearly the nature of the attempt to consider death an incident in human life rather than its termination."[54]

Kierkegaard would have none of this; or of the easy humanism that saw ethics as giving life meaning, ignoring the despair before death of even ethical paragons. "Is then the only conclusion that human existence can be only existence in tragedy and despair?" Drucker asks.

> Kierkegaard has another answer: human existence is possible as existence not in despair, as existence not in tragedy; it is possible as existence in faith. . . . Faith is the belief that in God the impossible is possible, that in Him time and eternity are one, that both life and death are meaningful.

Peter Drucker is a worldly philosopher. "[M]y work has been totally in society—except for this essay on Kierkegaard." But the passage above does more than reveal his spiritual hunger. It illumines his social thought. Finding meaning may not after all be possible within society. Drucker locates it in a faith that transcends society. That may also be where the members of his new society will have to find it—in faith, not, as Drucker hoped in his early books, in work. Drucker never washes his hands of this vale of tears, however, never lets his spiritual convictions stop him from working toward the bungalow Utopia of the "bearable society."[55]

# 6

# Inventing Management

ON OR about November 6, 1954, Peter Drucker invented management. His timing was felicitous: the "management boom" of the 1950s and 1960s was set to go off, yet there was no book to herald it, no book to explain management to managers, no book to establish management as among the major social innovations of the twentieth century. Drucker would supply the lack.

While researching *Concept of the Corporation,* Drucker asked GM executives if they could point him toward authorities on their obscure profession. "I kept hearing about Harry Hopf," he told Warren Bennis.

He was an insurance consultant and had built a library which became the nucleus of the General Electric Management Institute in Crotonville, New York. So I went out to visit Mr. Hopf, who was an elderly gentleman and ailing. He had the biggest management library in the world. The *only* one. His library was an enormous room with thousands and thousands of volumes. My heart fell when I saw it. He said to me, "Young man, I understand that you are interested in management." And I said, "Yes sir." He said, "There are only six books here about management. The rest are all about insurance, selling, advertising, and manufacturing."

It turned out that three of them weren't quite management. So *practically nothing* existed.[1]

To be sure management existed before Drucker made it conscious of itself. However, like the character in Molière who spoke prose without knowing it, for the most part managers managed without knowing what they were doing or what they should be doing. Early prototypes of the manager included the overseer driving slaves for plantation owners in the South and the superintendent keeping a flinty eye on textile workers in Northern factories. However, "The best-kept secret in management," Drucker writes, "is that the first systematic applications of management theory and management principles did not take place in business enterprise. They occurred in the public sector" in the reorganization of the US Army by Elihu Root, Theodore Roosevelt's secretary of war. One of the first "managed" organizations in America, also in the public sector, was the Second Bank of the United States, Alfred D. Chandler reports in *The Visible Hand,* his monumental history of "The Managerial Revolution in American Business." It was by far the biggest bank in the country, with twenty-two branches. Yet it took only three men to manage it, Nicholas Biddle, its president, and his two assistants. "The volume of business carried on by the biggest and most powerful financial institution of the day," Chandler writes, "was not yet large enough to require the creation of a managerial hierarchy."[2]

That kind of volume came only with the railroads. The railroads were not like plantations or factories. Their heavy capital costs required financing by more than one owner. Moreover, on account of their scale, they had to be operated by men who were not their owners— America's first managers.

By the 1890s the railroads were the biggest businesses, the biggest social entities, in the country: In 1891, when the Pennsylvania Railroad employed over 100,000 workers, there were only 39,000 men in the whole of the armed forces. Running these sprawling roads required an elaborate management hierarchy, which became the model for subsequent corporate enterprises.[3]

As late as the early 1940s, Mr. Hopf had just three management books in his library because management had yet to emerge as an integrating discipline in its own right. It was a palette of expertise drawn from engineering, accounting, sales, psychology, labor relations, and military formulary. Books purporting to be about management predictably reminded Drucker "of a book on human anatomy that would discuss one joint in the body—the elbow, for instance—without even mentioning the arm, let alone the skeleton."[4]

Since the publication of *Concept of the Corporation,* Drucker's consulting practice had grown to include giants like Sears, Roebuck, the Chesapeake & Ohio Railroad, and General Electric; but wherever he went Drucker found a "near-total absence of study, thought and knowledge regarding the job, function and challenges of management. . . ." Explaining the origins of his first management book, Drucker says, "I wanted something that would give the managers I worked with in my client companies *everything* they would need to do their jobs and prepare themselves for top-management responsibility . . ."[5]

To judge by a sample of the reviews, he succeeded handsomely. Writing in the *Saturday Review,* Alexander R. Heron, while adjudging Drucker's prose as "nothing to read for relaxation"(!) was justly generous towards Drucker's accomplishment: "The serious reader of *The Practice of Management* cannot fail to gain a concept that is nothing short of a new faith. . . . The hundreds of authors of other books on management owe a debt of gratitude to Peter Drucker. He may blast their theses . . . But in one volume he has given universal meaning to their efforts (and) lasting value to their interest in this new institution, Management." *Business Week* noted that "[T]here is very little print on the job of the manager as a whole. . . . Now Peter F. Drucker, teacher and consultant, has swept the field with *The Practice of Management.* Like many a pioneer in the arts and sciences, it is sure to be followed by many others. But it is likely to be the best of its kind for a long time to come."

"When I published *Practice of Management,*" Drucker told a skeptical interviewer, "that book made it possible for people to learn how to manage, something that up until then only a few geniuses seemed able to do, and nobody could replicate it. I sat down and made a discipline of it."

Q: Well you didn't invent the stuff.
A: In large part, yes.

Drucker added this Clintonesque clarification: "Look, if you can't replicate something because you don't understand it, then it really hasn't been invented; it's only been done."[6]

In that sense, then, Peter Drucker invented management.

"THE MANAGER is the dynamic, life-giving element in every business." With that, Drucker launches his expedition through "the dark continent of management."[7]

Drucker wants his readers to regard management as an institution worth writing and reading about. An historian need not justify history in his third paragraph, but the first historian did. Thus Drucker begins with dramatic assertions of management's significance: "The emergence of management . . . a pivotal event in social history. . . . Management will remain a basic dominant institution perhaps as long as Western civilization itself survives. . . . Management expresses the basic beliefs of modern Western society. . . . It is the organ of society explicitly charged with making resources productive . . . it reflects the basic spirit of the modern age. . . . It is in fact indispensable." The pageant swells: "Management is not a creature of the economy; it is a creator as well." It "masters the economic circumstances and alters them by conscious directed action." It does not merely adapt to the "forces of the market," but "creates them by its own action."[8]

As for the manager, he is the bringer of life charged with creating a "true whole that is more than the sum of its parts," something that "is possible only in the moral sphere" which makes the manager a sort of moral alchemist. Cleansed as by an ordeal of ambition to be worthy of his powers, the manager leads by "integrity of character." "He commands more respect than does the most likeable man. He demands exacting workmanship. . . . He sets high standards. . . . He considers what is right and never who is right." The businessmen and bosses of American fiction and film—narrow, avaricious, mean—cannot be recognized in these heroic lineaments.[9]

To Drucker, Alan Kantrow surmises, the manager has this Promethean character because he stands between civilization and barbarism. "Drucker is so deeply concerned about the profession of management," Kantrow writes, "because he is profoundly afraid of what might happen if the major institutions of Western society fail in their essential responsibilities." Other writers on management "who are both younger in years and American by birth . . . can never share the shattering immediacy of his sense of the price paid by the twentieth century for institutional failure." Economic health depends on management performance; if it fails, if the economy should falter, history might repeat itself. The manager, for Drucker, is the culture hero of the twentieth century; our protector, in his words, from "the dark forces that lurk just beneath the thin veneer of civilization that we had thought to have repaired during and after World War II."[10]

Yet this guardian of civilization is largely unknown, goes uncelebrated. Management is "the least understood of our basic institutions." This is true even of people in business "who often do not know what their management does and what it is supposed to be doing, how it acts and why, whether it does a good job or not."[11]

"What then is management: what does it do?" Drucker rummages medical science for a metaphor. "Management is an organ; and organs can only be defined through their function." As "the specific organ of the business enterprise," management's first function is to manage a

---

### The Parable of the Three Stonecutters

Asked what they were doing,

—the first replied, "I am making a living"
—the second replied, "I am doing the best job of stonecutting in the country"
—the third replied, "I am building a cathedral."

The third man is, of course, the true "manager."

—*The Practice of Management* (1954)

---

business. Its second is to manage managers. Its third is to manage worker and work.[12]

DRUCKER BEGINS on the ground floor, with the question, "What is a business?" The answer usually given, "An organization to make a profit" is "not only false; it is irrelevant."[13]

Profit-seeking is not the cause of management decisions but the test of their validity. "If you want to know what a business is we have to start with its *purpose*," which must be found "outside the business itself . . . in society since a business enterprise is an organ of society." The drums roll, "There is only one valid definition of business purpose: *to create a customer.*" This is the Drucker dictum best known around the world. He jokes that his ideas "have only one moving part," which is why this one in particular has traveled so well.[14]

Drucker quickly gets practical about customers and the challenge of creating and keeping them, but first it is worth pausing over a phrase he lets slip in passing that reveals nothing less than the key to his whole social vision. He says, ". . . it is to supply the consumer that *society entrusts* [my italics] wealth-producing resources to the business enterprise." That is the type of similar formulations throughout his work; they express not so much the working assumptions of his thought as its moral starting point.

"Society entrusts." The atomistic individualism of contract theory, beloved of libertarian theorists, holds that society does not, cannot, entrust anything. Business undertakings, as most human relationships, are contracts between freely consenting individuals. "Society" is merely the aggregation of such individuals, with largely notional existence apart from them. To attribute powers to "Society" is atavistic, a return to the organic vision of the Middle Ages which it has been the business of classical economics to discredit.

Drucker, recall, differed from Karl Polanyi over the degree of autonomy the economy requires from society, not over the principle that society comes first and economy exists to serve it. In Drucker's worldview, society has historically "refused to allow . . . permanent concentrations of power, at least in private hands, and certainly for economic purposes." But an industrial society cannot exist without ceding such powers to the enterprise. "Hence society has been forced to grant the enterprise what it has always been reluctant to grant, that is, first a charter of perpetuity, if not of theoretical immortality to the "legal person," and second a degree of authority to the managers which corresponds to the needs of the enterprise."[15]

In contract theory, by pursuing his own selfish interests, a harmonics of virtue orchestrated by "the invisible hand" of the market leads the property owner automatically to serve the public good. In Drucker's neo-organic theory the invisible conscience takes the place of the invisible hand: the property owner, the man or woman of business, the managers of the modern enterprise must consciously "assume responsibility for the public good" and "restrain their self-interest and their authority wherever their exercise would infringe upon the commonweal and upon the freedom of the individual." This demanding conservative vision looks behind nineteenth-century liberalism to the *idea* of a social order infused with moral purpose, in which the acceptance of responsibilities, duties, and obligations justifies the assertion of rights.

Here is the touchstone of Drucker's thought. When he scores corporate acts as "antisocial," this is that judgment's ground. When he brands as "socially unforgivable" the practice of executives reaping financial gain for laying off workers, or when he calls for business to show greater "social responsibility," or declares that the industrial enterprise has "a duty to keep open the opportunity to rise from the bottom according to ability and performance," or says that the hostile takeover wave of the 1980s, "deeply offends the sense of justice of a great many Americans," his vision of society gives him the moral warrant. "Free enterprise," he writes, cadence making thought memorable, "cannot be justified as being good for business. It can be justified only as being good for society."[16]

After the failure of his quixotic hopes for *Concept of the Corporation,* Drucker, as noted, expects less from big business and big labor; his explicit vision narrows. But implicitly, and connected to no vulnerable programmatics like the self-governing plant community, Drucker's social idealism never leaves him. His criticism of market capitalism and its theoretical rationale remains fundamental. "Capitalism," he writes at the end of *The Practice of Management,* "is being attacked not because it is inefficient or misgoverned but because it is cynical. And indeed a society based on the assertion that private vices become public benefits cannot endure, no matter how impeccable its logic, no matter how great its benefits."[17]

First and last, Peter Drucker is a moralist of our business civilization. And just as we don't read George Orwell for his answers to the social and political problems he explores but for his moral clarity and depth, so we don't come to Drucker looking for three-point plans to fix creation. He offers suggestions, he affirms the values at stake, sometimes he points in the right direction; but he offers few solutions and those he does offer he intends as no more than notes toward a solution. Montaigne offered no solutions, either. It is enough for the moralist to mark the distance between what is and what could be.

\*    \*    \*

DRUCKER WAS about to tell us how to manage a business. To ask, "What is our business?"; "What will be our business?"; and "What should be our business?" Drucker's "three classic queries," according to The American Banker, is the first function of management. The first question "looks so simple that it is seldom raised, the answer seems so obvious that it is seldom given." Yet, failure to ask it "is the most important single cause of business failure."[18]

Drucker gives an example of the question's unexpected power when asked by someone like Theodore N. Vail, the builder of AT&T, which early in the twentieth century turned to Vail to save it from foundering. He began by scrapping AT&T's traditional answer to the first question, What is our business?, which was to sell, install, and charge for the use of telephones. Fearful that his "natural monopoly" would be nationalized, the fate of telephone systems throughout Europe and Canada, and sensing that attacking public ownership as "socialistic" or "un-American" would be a losing battle, Vail repositioned AT&T with a new statement of its mission: "Our business is service."[19]

AT&T's business was to give its customers service, which meant that it could no longer behave like a monopoly. It had to train its employees accordingly: "Vail saw to it that the yardsticks throughout the system by which managers and their operations were judged, measured service fulfillment rather than profit performance." AT&T also had to invest in research—the famed Bell Labs—to constantly improve its service and innovate new products. It had to emphasize service in its advertising and public relations. And it had to accept and work with government *regulation,* infinitely preferable to government control, not resist it. By taking steps like these, Vail intuitively sensed, AT&T would both please customers and change the political environment, obviating any thought of nationalizing such a consumer-friendly corporation.[20]

And, Drucker wants us to understand, AT&T was a "successful business." In starting a business, the question "What is our business?" is frivolous. "The man who mixes up a new cleaning fluid and peddles it door to door . . ." is not about to ask what he's doing and why.

> But when the product catches on; when he has to hire people to mix it and to sell it; when he has to decide whether to keep on selling it directly or through retail shops, whether through department stores, supermarkets, hardware stores or through all three; what additional products he needs for a full "line"—then he has to ask and to answer the question: "what is my business?" If he fails to answer it when successful, he will, even with the best of products, soon be back wearing out his own shoe leather peddling from door to door.[21]

The thick circumstantiality of that passage, its fluidity and deftness of specification, is characteristic of the writing in *The Practice of Management,* Drucker's most impressive book by virtue of the energies of discovery it released in him. If Drucker's thematic books on Big Questions are short on evidence, his management books bulge with disguised evidence (as a rule, Drucker does not reveal the names of his clients) drawn from his consulting practice. Asked how he uses his consulting in his management books, he says, "I steal." His readers gain from the theft.[22]

Management's second function is to manage managers. Drucker begins with one of his favorite cautionary examples from business history.

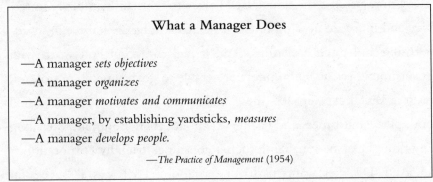

**What a Manager Does**

—A manager *sets objectives*
—A manager *organizes*
—A manager *motivates and communicates*
—A manager, by establishing yardsticks, *measures*
—A manager *develops people.*

*—The Practice of Management* (1954)

Henry Ford nearly destroyed his business by trying to run the Ford Motor Company without managers. The old man sought to manage a billion dollar business by himself. "The secret police that spied on all Ford executives served to inform Henry Ford of any attempt on the part of one of his executives to make a decision." Only the bold postwar reorganization by Ford's grandson, Henry Ford II, saved the "nearly bankrupt" company. He brought the managerial revolution to Ford, replacing, "The concept of the executive as a personal delegate of the owner . . . [with] the concept of the manager whose authority is grounded in the objective responsibility of the job."[23]

Managers cannot supervise *other* managers; Ford the elder showed what happens when they try. Instead, they must "manage by objectives," Drucker's second most famous dictum (he wrote a book about it ten years after *The Practice of Management*). Basically, managing by objectives changes the job of the manager from supervising subordinates to setting with them objective measures and goals, leaving them to achieve them as they will. These agreed yardsticks allow the managed manager, in turn, to manage by objectives and self-control, that is, "to appraise himself . . . rather than be appraised and controlled from the outside."

"Management by objectives" (MBO in shorthand) may seem a counsel of the obvious today, but it was far from obvious when Drucker introduced it in 1954. "If anything," *The Economist* notes, "Mr. Drucker's very success is an obstacle to appreciating his importance. Many of his most innovative ideas have become commonplaces." Managing by objectives is "the dominant concept in management today," according to the management writer John J. Tarrant. "This idea is thought by a good many people to be the most important and influential concept Drucker has ever generated." Richard H. Buskirk, of the School of Business Administration at Southern Methodist University brings out its Copernican effect: "His emphasis upon the results of managerial actions rather than the supervision of activities was a major contribution for it shifted the entire focus of management thought to productivity—output—and away from work efforts—input."

Drucker cites General Electric as a model of managing by objectives and self-control. GE conducted a yearly audit of each of its managerial units. But instead of sending its findings to top management, GE sent them to the unit managers. "There can be little doubt," Drucker writes, "that the feeling of confidence and trust in the company which even casual contact with General Electric managers reveals is traceable to this practice of using information for self-control rather than control from above." One of GE's divisions expressed the company philosophy in this provision of its charter: "All authority not expressly and in writing reserved for higher management is granted to lower management."[24]

W. Edwards Deming, the father of the "quality revolution" in American business and Drucker's one-time colleague at New York University, thought MBO was hostile to quality because it was goal-focused, not process-focused: it dealt with ends not means. An organization can resort to any means to accomplish virtually any end it wants, short term. It can, for example, show a profit "if it juggles the books and sells off its healthiest operations," to use the summary of Deming's views by Andrea Gabor, a Deming biographer. Reading Drucker's "objectives" as "quotas," Deming said: "A quota is a fortress against improvement of quality and productivity. I have yet to see a quota that includes any trace of a system by which to help anyone to do a better job." As an example Deming cites the policeman who must issue a quota of parking tickets every day: this is what MBO can mean. In fairness Drucker was primarily concerned with establishing the distinction between MBO and management by supervision; that was the main purpose of the concept. Replacing supervision, MBO would lead to an overarching goal Drucker and Deming shared: a nonauthoritarian workplace, a setting far more congenial to quality than what it replaced.

Finally, in hiring a manager, the manager of managers must look above all for "integrity." That may be hard to define, Drucker says, "but what constitutes lack of integrity of such seriousness as to disqualify a man is not." Drucker recommends the Miss Sophy test to measure his special idea of integrity: "A man should never be appointed to a managerial position if his vision focuses on people's weaknesses rather than on their strengths." Drucker sees integrity as a kind of social faith—as residing in a generous attitude toward other people's possibilities and a leniency toward their limitations. There is a human warmth to his moral intelligence, an acceptance of fallibility and a canny appreciation of its uses. "The better a man is," he writes, "the more mistakes will he make—for the more new things he will try. I would never promote a man into a top-level job who had not made mistakes, and big ones at that. Otherwise he is sure to be mediocre."[25]

The credo the manager of managers should live by is emblazoned on Andrew Carnegie's tombstone:

> Here lies a man
> Who knew how to enlist
>  In his service
> Better men than himself

Manage more managers than you really ought to, Drucker advises managers, to stop yourself from acting the supervisor and gelding your managers into clerks.[26]

MANAGEMENT'S THIRD function is to manage worker and work. Here Drucker's example is another of his big clients of the 1940s and 1950s, IBM.

IBM wins Drucker's praise by enlarging its jobs, giving each worker scope and challenge, among other morale-enhancing policies. The key IBM innovation, however, is its employment strategy. IBM seeks to maintain stable employment to enable its employees to contribute their maximum effort without fear of "working themselves out of a job." At least one major American company had grasped the point of *Concept of the Corporation.* Even during the worst of the Depression, IBM held on to its people. To keep them working, IBM had to develop new markets for its products. Employment policy dictated basic corporate strategy. "It is not correct to say that we managed to maintain employment during the Depression because we grew" an IBM executive told Drucker. "We grew because we had committed ourselves to the maintenance of employment. This forced us to find new users and new uses for our existing products . . . to find unsatisfied wants in the market and to develop new products to satisfy them . . . to develop foreign markets and to push export sales." Alas for changing times, what the Depression could not do, competitive pressure from the world market has done: force IBM to lay off thousands.[27]

"We cannot sit back and expect worker motivation to arise spontaneously, now that fear is gone," Drucker writes of the biggest challenge of managing worker and work. "To eliminate [fear] has been the main result of the increased wealth produced by industrialization. In a society rich enough to provide sustenance even to the unemployed, fear has lost its motivating power." Note the apolitical, ahistorical spin there: industrialization banished fear, not the social and political responses to it—from laws regulating wages and hours to the liberal/labor politics of the New Deal.[28]

Finding sources of positive motivation to replace fear is "one of the most urgent tasks facing management." Throughout his work, Drucker brushes aside material incentives (an attitude that may spring from his awareness of his own motives: money cannot be a deciding motive for a man who has been donating half his consulting time to nonprofit groups for fifty years). The nineteenth-century factory worker may have had only economic goals, Drucker argues, but that "ceased to be true the moment pay went above the subsistence level," a Spartan idea of human wants and wishes. Today's "knowledge worker," a Drucker coinage, also has economic demands. The absence of economic satisfactions is a deterrent for the knowledge worker, Drucker writes in *The Effective Executive* (1966). "But their presence is not enough. He needs opportunity, he needs achievement, he needs fulfillment, he needs values." Where the manual laborer expected "a living from work, the knowledge worker expects a life out of it."[29]

Managers can demand two things from workers: dedication to their jobs and the willingness "to accept change." Management must be able to innovate in designing work and in matching worker and job. Change will be resisted, however, if it threatens the worker's "psychological security; and man being mortal, frail and limited, his security is always precarious—" which, in an era of rapid economic and technological change, means job security. To accept change, the worker needs something in return. IBM showed the way; openness to innovation requires the real, not just psychological, security of stable employment. In today's harsher climate, the worker must accept change with *no* promise of security from its consequences.[30]

Drucker has a withering chapter on Personnel Management, the school of management thought that seeks positive motivations to work. "Some wit once said maliciously that it puts together and calls personnel management all those things that do not deal with the work of people and that are not management" which sounds a lot like Drucker quoting Drucker. The cardinal error personnel managers

---

### How to Manage the Boss: The "Dos and Don'ts"

"The Dos

"Once a year ask the boss, 'What do I or my people do that helps you to do your job?' and 'What do I or my people do that hampers you?'

"The subordinate's job is not to reform or reeducate the boss, not to make him conform to what the business schools or the management book say bosses should be like. It is to enable a particular boss to perform as a unique individual.

"A manager's task is to make the strengths of people effective and their weaknesses irrelevant—and that applies fully as much to the manager's boss as it applies to the manager's subordinates.

"Keep the boss aware. Bosses, after all, are held responsible by their own bosses for the performance of their subordinates. They must be able to say: 'I know what Anne [or Joe] is trying to do.'

"The Don'ts

"Never expose the boss to surprises—even pleasant ones (if any such exist). To be exposed to a surprise in the organization one is responsible for is humiliation, and usually public humiliation.

"Never underrate the boss! The boss may look illiterate. He may look stupid. But there is no risk at all in overrating a boss. If you underrate him he will bitterly resent it or impute to you the deficiency in brains and knowledge you imputed to him."

—*Managing for the Future* (1992)

---

commit is philosophical: they assume people don't want to work and must be manipulated to work. Nothing good can flow from any policy based on that assumption, says Drucker, who believes that people not only want to work and to achieve in work; they *need* to work. "Most people disintegrate morally and physically if they do not work."[31]

The human relations school, which uses a therapeutic approach to worker motivation, is only marginally better than the personnel management school. "It freed management from the domination of viciously wrong ideas; but it did not succeed in substituting new concepts." Human relations focuses on individual psychology and interpersonal relations in the workplace. "As a result, it assumes that it is immaterial what kind of work a man does since it is only his relation to his fellow men that determines his behavior and his effectiveness." Moreover, Drucker adds, human relations easily degenerates into a device "to 'sell' whatever management is doing." (That might also be said of "the managerial attitude.") "It is no accident that there is so much talk in human relations about 'giving workers a sense of responsibility' and so little about their responsibility, so much emphasis on their 'feeling of importance' and so little on making them and their work important." These sly suasions illustrate the change in management technique in the postwar era, to quote Daniel Bell, "from authority to manipulation as a means of exercising dominion."[32]

The ruling concept of how to manage worker and work, however, is Lenin's favorite method, "Scientific Management" or "Taylorism" after its father, the time-and-motion study man, Frederick W. Taylor (1856–1915). As a boy Taylor counted his steps while walking to school to discover his most efficient stride. "He couldn't stand the sight of an idle lathe or an idle man," Bell writes. "He never loafed, and he was going to make sure that nobody else did."[33]

To Drucker, this Moses of efficiency is an unsung hero of prosperity: "Scientific Management was one of the great liberating, pioneering insights." The scientific analysis of the minutest motions of the simplest work made mass production, and especially its assembly-line form, possible. This in turn made what Drucker calls "The Productivity Revolution," to which we owe our dinners, possible. All this may be so, but it is willfully contrarian to call the science behind the *assembly line* a "liberating . . . insight."[34]

Drucker rounds on himself to deplore the separation between thinking and doing at the core of Taylorism:

> It does not follow from the separation of planning and doing in the analysis of work that the planner and doer should be two different people. It does not follow that the industrial world should be divided into

two classes of people: a few who decide what is to be done, design the job, set the pace, rhythm and motions, and order others about; and the many who do what and as they are told.

It does not follow; but it has followed. Needed is a Taylorism of the qualitative, Drucker says, an understanding of work that values "the special properties of the human being, that is, his ability to make a whole of many things, to judge, to plan, and to change." Drucker was hopeful that the years would bring this understanding; no doubt he still is.[35]

Drucker's candidate to replace fear, manipulation, and the tyranny of the stopwatch as methods of managing workers and work is his aristocratic standard of "Responsibility." Essentially this means extending downward the management by self-control used to manage managers. "It does not matter whether the worker wants responsibility or not," Drucker writes, his voice uncharacteristically hard. "The enterprise must demand it of him." The worker must match his performance against the highest standard possible—his own.[36]

This idea has troubling resonances. As Drucker argued in *The Effective Executive* (1966), CEOs must manage themselves, managers of managers must manage themselves, managers must manage themselves, and even workers, it appears, must manage themselves. "The worker does not need praise or reproach to know how he is doing. He knows." Drucker's solution to the motivation problem is to empower the superego, to set people loose against their own human tendencies to be satisfied with sloppy work, to waste time, chew the fat, daydream about their lovers, worry about their kids, plan the next camping trip—in short, to show that they do not take their jobs all that seriously all the time. Most people don't, and many can't. In his journal *Eupsychian Management,* the famed psychiatrist Abraham Maslow criticized the concept of the Responsible Worker as a counsel of perfection. (Ever fair-minded, Drucker has tried to get Maslow's book reprinted for years.)

> Drucker talks much about "responsibility" and the liking for responsibil-
> ity and cites all sorts of industrial investigations that show people function
> better when they get responsibility. This is certainly true but only for the
> more mature, more healthy [sic] person whom Drucker assumes through-
> out. But point out that this kind of person is not universal. . . . It is clear
> that we must be more conscious than Drucker that this is . . . a selection
> out of particular kinds of people.

As teacher, writer, consultant, Drucker is responsible about his work; he takes it seriously, because it *is* serious. Can any amount of "responsibility," however, redeem the making of lamp shades and light bulbs for seriousness? The concept of the responsible worker sacrifices individual to social character by giving work an existential intensity it cannot, perhaps should not, bear. After all, Kierkegaard teaches, we owe only provisional loyalty to the provisional, saving our absolute loyalty for the absolute.[37]

IN TRYING to place Drucker's major books of the 1950s: *The New Society, The Practice of Management,* and *Landmarks of the Future* in their time, one is struck by the difficulty of the placing. In general outlook they diverge sharply from one of the strongest currents in the culture of the era—preoccupation of many intellectuals with the growth of "conformity" in American society. Once politically radical intellectuals were no longer engaged by issues of economic justice (a third of Americans were still poor) or social justice (Jim Crow still ruled the South) but with what David Riesman, in *The Lonely Crowd,* termed "the malaise of affluence." "On the Exhaustion of Political

Ideas in the 1950s," the subtitle of Daniel Bell's *The End of Ideology*, signaled the new mood. Like a "herd of independent minds," in Harold Rosenberg's memorable estimation, the "New York Intellectuals," the twelve or fifteen writers through whom later generations know the 1950s, looked with alarm at conformity and, when they didn't blame it on the mass media, blamed it on something equally new pervading American society—the organization. Popular novels (and movies) like Sloan Wilson's *The Man in the Grey Flannel Suit,* nonfiction best sellers like William H. Whyte's *The Organization Man,* and works of social science like *The Lonely Crowd* and *Individualism Reconsidered,* depicted the large organization as cold, impersonal, intolerant of individuality, a graveyard for creativity, imagination, and autonomy—an alien life-sucking force altogether. He had a new appreciation of the old-time "boss," Whyte wrote after his reporting on the human desert of the corporation. The boss only asked for "your sweat"; the organization "asked for your soul."[38]

Mark the chasm from Drucker: "Organization is the specific instrument to make human strengths [redound] to performance while human weakness is neutralized and largely rendered harmless." What the intellectuals saw as anxiety-haunted conformity, he saw as task-driven cooperation. ("Morale in an organization," he writes, "does not mean that 'people get along together'; the test is performance not conformance.") The intellectuals pictured the organization as a kind of prison; he pictured it as a kind of community. What they saw as spiritually deadening, he saw as liberating. If they made organizational life out to be worse than it was, he made it out to be better. If they projected what they were against on the organization, he projected what he was for. If they feared the encroachments of society on the individual, he feared the encroachments of economy on society. To the intellectuals the organization was the problem; to Drucker it was the solution—and not only to the frustration of human potential through all history, but also to anomie, the rule-less individualism of the criminal, the man living beyond moral appeal.[39]

For Drucker, cooperation within an organization has an "intrinsic morality" of its own. The words belong to Emile Durkheim, who saw the "organic solidarity" wrought by work based on the division of labor—work, that is, in common and through an organization—as the source of morality in the modern age. "Everything which is a source of solidarity is moral," Durkheim writes, "everything which forces man to take account of other men is moral, everything which forces him to regulate his conduct through something other than the striving of his own ego is moral, and morality is as solid as these ties are numerous and strong." This view of society and its little platoon, the organization, is Drucker writ sociologically.

If you believe that the organization expands human capacity and opportunity as no other work of man has ever done before; and if you also believe that the organization fosters morality by nothing it makes but by its thick sociality of cooperation, then you are unlikely to see conformity as a social problem or the organization as a thief of men's souls. "The fundamental reality for every worker, from sweeper to executive vice-president," Drucker writes with trumping concreteness, "is the eight hours or so he spends on the job. In our society of organizations, it is the job through which the great majority has access to achievement, to fulfillment, and to community."[40]

BY THE end of the 1950s Drucker no longer had to justify the manager and management. He could instead turn to mundane practicalities. This he did in *Managing for Results* (1964). Leaner and less exalted than *The Practice of Management,* it is the only book of Drucker's to contain charts.

The original title was "Business Strategies," but after both author and publisher tried it on people with business experience, the title was rejected. "Strategy," we were told again and again, "belongs to military or perhaps to political campaigns but not to business." Strategy has since become a lucrative cliché of business book titles. But Drucker still prefers *Managing for Results.* It has the one moving part, which helps an idea to catch on. "Above all, it expresses the book's premise: businesses exist to produce results on the outside, in the market and the economy."[41]

*Managing for Results* begins with an inventory of "business realities"—the demands of "outside" that the business executive has to consider as 'givens,' as constants, as challenges."

Drucker presents eight of these realities.

1. *Resources and results exist outside not inside the business.* Knowledge, "a universal social resource," is outside, meaning that any technological edge a business may have over its competitors is fleeting. The customer, too, is outside. "Results depend not on anybody within the business nor on anything within the control of the business."

2. *Results come from exploiting opportunities, not from solving problems.* "All one can hope to get by solving a problem is to restore normality." Opportunities, meanwhile, go unexploited. The distinction between problems and opportunities is one of Drucker's conceptual coups. He applies it repeatedly to executives who "operate," jump from problem to problem, when their job is to seize opportunities.

3. *For results, resources must go to opportunities, not to problems.*

4. *"Economic results" do not go to minor players in a given market, but to leaders.* "Unless it has . . . a leadership position, a business, a product, a service, becomes marginal. . . ." It is either lead or fail; Drucker explains why in detail.

5. *Leadership, however, is not likely to last.* "Business tends to drift from leadership to mediocrity." The executive must sense inchoate erosion and correct it by steering the company away from problems and toward new opportunities.

6. *"What exists is getting old."* Past decisions, policies, strategies need to be revisited, challenged, made to justify themselves in terms of the challenge of the new.

7. *What exists is likely to be misallocated.* The first 10 percent of efforts may account for as much as 90 percent of results. Meaning 90 percent of efforts are going for naught and could be applied elsewhere.

8. *To achieve economic results, concentrate.* Real achievement is possible only in a few areas. Beware diffusion of effort. Focus resources to meet only the "decisive opportunities."[42]

There are more lists like this in *Managing for Results,* but they are not meant for civilian eyes. Drucker displays some rare lapses into professionalese in regrettable displays like: "One reason is the common management mistake of identifying profit margin with profit which is always profit margin multiplied by turnover"; and, "One should actually stop further inputs before the output gain for each incremental input unit starts to go down."

Sentences like that should endear Drucker to management academics, whose language this is, but that does not appear to be the case. In eighteen years of teaching at a leading management school, one professor told me, he had never assigned a Drucker book nor seen a colleague assign a Drucker book nor knew of professors at other institutions who assigned Drucker books. "We do empirical research," he said. "Drucker stays in his office and thinks"—if you can imagine *that.* Tom Peters, coauthor of *In Search of Excellence,* says he earned two graduate degrees in business school without ever studying Drucker. Yet Peters also says that "everything we had written" in *In Search of Excellence* could be found "in some corner or other" of the *Practice of Management.* When I called a business school dean to inquire about Drucker's influence on management (as distinguished from schools of management), he told me that Drucker had made an historic contribution. "Management has evolved from four routes," he said: "the

Florentine bankers invent accounting, Frederick Taylor invents scientific management, Albert P. Sloan and decentralization in the 1920s—and Peter Drucker in the postwar period, notably his work on organization and strategy." Indicative, perhaps, of a new academic interest in Drucker, a very recent business school textbook credits him, along with others, for propelling "the notion of strategy into the forefront of management practice." Neither this nor a later favorable citation bothers to identify Drucker, the authors assuming that graduate school students already know who he is.[43]

The actual discussion of strategy in *Managing for Results* is relatively brief; one had expected more from Drucker's retrospective representations. It deals with such questions as, What are the pros and cons of pursuing a diversification as opposed to a specialization strategy? How big should my business be? The small business, the medium-size business, the large business: what are the problems of each that stem primarily from size?

The *Effective Executive* (1966) is Newt Gingrich's favorite Drucker book. At least one reason why is obvious. Anybody who has to sit through marathon meetings will love this book and stick thrusts like this on the office billboard: "[O]ne either meets or one works . . ."[45]

*The Effective Executive* is Drucker's most enjoyable management book, full of one-liners and written with cleverness and pleasure in its exercise.

Drucker begins with yet another of his dyads: the difference between doing the right thing and getting the right thing done. The former is the standard of efficiency applied to manual work. The latter is the standard of *effectiveness:* The effective executive gets the right things done.[44]

Effectiveness, Drucker writes, does not correlate with intelligence or imagination. Plodders can be effective, while creative types famously can't get anything *done*. Nor is there "an effective personality." From Alfred P. Sloan forward the executives Drucker has observed "shared nothing in common except the ability to get the right things done." "Effectiveness . . . is a habit; that is, a complex of practices. And practices can always be learned." *The Effective Executive* is a manual on how to be effective.[46]

Effective executives live by the credo "Know Thy Time." They do not start with their tasks; "They start with their time." They manage time, the scarcest of all human resources, by, for example, "consolidating it into the largest possible continuing units"; and also by delegating everything that can be delegated. If the task will not have "irreversible impact" on the enterprise, then it can be delegated.[47]

Effective executives focus on *results,* which are outside, in the mercurial world of the customer, not on *work,* which happens inside. Periodically, they put to themselves another patented Drucker question: "What can I contribute that will significantly affect the performance and the results of the institution I serve?" The emphasis on contribution puts the executive's unique gifts first in contrast to, "What work should I do?," which puts the work first.[48]

Effective executives "do not build on weakness. They do not start out with the things they cannot do." They build on strength. They never ask, "How does he get along with me?" They ask instead, "What does he contribute?" They understand that to try to build on weakness, or to suppose that everyone should be good at everything, is to violate the purpose of organization.[49]

Effective executives do "first things first—and second things not at all." They recognize their situation between two conflicting flows of time—between the future, where results are, and the past, where problems are. To make room for the future, they "slough off yesterday" by asking, "If we did not already do this, would we go into it now?"— and abandoning anything to which the answer is "no." Abandonment, concededly, is a politically difficult undertaking, since the past dominates inside and the pressures from inside "always favor what has happened over the future, the crisis over the opportunity, the immediate and visible over the real, and the urgent over the relevant."[50]

Effective executives make effective decisions. They distinguish between the recurrent and the unique event. Policy can take care of the former; they decide the unique cases. They think through what's right before the compromises and accommodations "needed to make the decision acceptable. They build into the decision "the action to carry it out." Finally, they test their decision by its results. And they never make a decision without some disagreement.

In today's "information-based organization" the executive as general is losing ground to the executive as lead player in a jazz combo—or opera conductor. "The conductor of an opera has a very large number of different groups that he has to pull together," Drucker told *Forbes* in 1997. "The soloists, the chorus, the ballet, the orchestra, all have to come together—but they have a common score. What we are increasingly talking about today are diversified groups that have to write the score while they perform. . . . What you really need now is a good jazz group. . . . So how can you have a big company or a very big

---

### The Four Questions Asked by Effective Executives in Making People Decisions

"What has he [or she] done well?"

"What, therefore, is he likely to be able to do well?"

"What does he have to learn or acquire to be able to get the full benefit from his strength?"

"If I had a son or daughter, would I be willing to have him or her work under this person?"

(i) "If yes, why?"

(ii) "If no, why?"

—*The Effective Executive* (1966)

organization when you have to develop the score as you go along? Today you build different teams. Sounds beautiful. Yet nobody has really found a way to do it."

Drucker concludes *The Effective Executive* with a warning to the executives: beware the computer. It can expand the range of the executive effectiveness, but it also has a counter-tendency to isolate the executive from outside, to focus him on data, not on the business realities. Executives should model themselves on Alfred P. Sloan, who regularly dropped in on GM's car dealerships and service centers. "The danger is that executives will become contemptuous of information and stimulus that cannot be reduced to computer logic and computer language." And the computer's main defect can't be fixed: "The strength of the computer lies in its being a logic machine," Drucker writes. "It does precisely what it is programmed to do. This makes it fast and precise. It also makes it a total moron; for logic is essentially stupid." Still, with computation handed over to machines, "people way down the line in the organization will have to learn how to be executives and to make effective decisions," Drucker wrote in 1966, when computers were about the size of power generating plants. George Orwell once said that Shakespeare's social imagination was such that he could deduce the whole of Victorian England from a railway timetable. Drucker would need only a few more clues.[51]

IN THE mid-1940s, when Drucker first became interested in management, he could find only two companies, Sears, Roebuck and Marks & Spencer, the British retailer, that sought to develop managers. Only three universities had continuing advanced education programs for managers: New York University's Graduate Business School, where Drucker taught managers and professionals from banking and finance; the Sloan Program at the Massachusetts Institute of Technology; and the Advanced Management Program at the Harvard Business School.

Ten years later one survey revealed, 3,000 companies had manager development programs, and scores of universities, growing to hundreds by the late 1960s, gave graduate degrees in management.[52]

"The change from neglect of management to, first, awareness of and then to stress on management came as a result of World War II," Drucker says. "It was, above all, the performance of American manufacturing industry during the war that drew attention to management." The postwar Marshall Plan, which "set out to mobilize management for economic and social reconstruction . . . made management a bestseller." Management had directed the greatest industrial surge in history *and* the restoration of the war-ravaged European economy, creating a "management boom" of interest and emulation that ended only in the early 1970s.[53]

"What happened was that the mystique of management was suddenly gone." Highly visible business debacles of the late 1960s—Penn Central, Lockheed, Rolls-Royce—"made professional management look somewhat less than heroic." More critically, management had outgrown its aging knowledge base from the war. "New knowledge, new basic approaches, and new understanding, it was beginning to be seen, were needed. And those the management boom could not supply."[54]

The time was propitious for Peter Drucker to renew management by distilling the learning and reflection of decades into a book whose bulk and multitudinousness would serve to buoy the morale of a now middle-aged institution testing new challenges. In 1973, just as the OPEC oil cartel was quadrupling oil prices, levying a growth-slowing tax on the economies of the industrial world, Drucker published an 840-page monument of reassurance: *Management: Tasks, Responsibilities, Practices.*

In *Practice of Management* Drucker promised to tell the manager "everything" he would need to know to enhance his performance. *Management* assiduously redeems that pledge, and partly in the *Practice of*

*Management's* own words: much of the book is a reworking of Drucker's three management books of the 1950s and 1960s.

"The most important reason for focusing on business management," Drucker writes in his opening chapter, "is that it is the success story of the century." That revealing sentence belongs at the head of this book. It is the quickest entry to Drucker's world; from it you can extrapolate the broad features of his thought. "The achievement of business management enables us today to promise—perhaps prematurely (and certainly rashly)—the abolition of . . . grinding poverty . . ." Advanced societies can afford mass higher education thanks to the economic surplus created by business management. That there is knowledge work for educated people to do and that we (in 1973) can assume social mobility instead of the social petrification of all previous societies—this historic achievement, too, we owe to the fertility and enterprise of business management. In sum, the invention of management "may be the pivotal event of our times. . . . Rarely in human history has an institution proven indispensable so quickly."[55]

But ahead lie three exigent challenges. The first is the challenge of increasing productivity the hard way. Writing before the Arab Oil Boycott, which followed the Yom Kippur war between Israel and its Arab neighbors, Drucker, as usual, was ahead of events. The main engine of postwar growth, Drucker says, was the worldwide infusion into the industrial work force of people from low productivity agricultural areas. Japan, for example, went from having 60 percent of its population on the land in 1946 to less than 10 percent by the 1970s. But this was a one-time-only phenomenon. Productivity increases will now have to flow from people already in the workforce; the relative productivity gains derived from turning farm laborers into machine operators belong to the past.[56]

The second new challenge posed to management is what Drucker calls "The Crisis of the Manual Worker." The big gainer in the industrial postwar economy, the blue-collar worker is now threatened by management's efforts to meet the productivity challenge posed by the world economy: that is, through education and technology, to increase the knowledge content of all work. After a period of egalitarian opportunity, when family background and the schoolmaster could not decide economic fate—when a young person not adept at school but capable and diligent at work could become a unionized industrial worker and enter the middle class, history has turned against experience-based blue-collar work. Writing in *The New Realities* at the beginning of the 1990s, Drucker predicts that the blue-collar worker will have shrunk "to where farmers are now, that is, to between 5 and 10 percent of the workforce" by 2010. Already, in California, knowledge workers make up 25 percent of the workforce—the same percentage as blue-collar workers.

The fall of the blue-collar worker is really less a management challenge and more a social and political challenge. Drucker sees it affecting management by means of the blue-collar worker's fading union, which, through the demagoguery of decline will prove as big an irritant to management as strong unions once proved a threat. A weak union "does not mean management strength; it means management frustration."[57]

Worse, for society, than weak unions is no unions for a host of reasons. With the slippage of union representation of the private sector work force from 35 percent in the mid-1950s to barely 10 percent today, the social mobility Drucker (and America) took for granted in 1973, at the end of a period when real wages rose 2 percent a year, has since vanished as the crisis of the blue-collar worker has widened to include more and more pink- and white-collar workers. One statistic tells the story: the median weekly earnings of full-time male workers has dropped 13 percent since 1979.[58]

The third new challenge facing management is that of measuring and raising the productivity of knowledge work. A *New Yorker* cartoon captures the dilemma. It shows an office door with the legend: CHAS. SMITH, GENERAL SALES MANAGER, AJAX SOAP COM-PANY. The walls are bare except for a big sign saying THINK. The man in his office has his feet propped up on his desk and is blowing smoke rings at the ceiling. Outside two older men walk by, one saying to the other, "But how can we be sure that Smith is thinking *soap?*" Frederick Taylor could measure the productivity of a laborer shoveling sand; measuring what Smith is doing is not so easy. "One thing is clear," Drucker writes, "making knowledge productive will bring about changes in job structure, careers, and organization as drastic as those which resulted in the factory from the application of scientific management to manual work." That *sounds* like a prevision of reengineering twenty years before the reality.[59]

In the architectonics of Drucker's thought, *Management* answers a question first raised in *The Future of Industrial Man* and characterized there as haunting managerial capitalism: the question of the legitimacy of managerial authority in an age when owners don't (and can't) run big corporations. "Legitimate is a power when it is justified by an eth-ical or metaphysical principle that has been accepted by society," Drucker wrote in *Industrial Man*. In the modern corporation the power of its managers, "derived from no one but from the managers them-selves," lacked legitimacy—it was "unfounded, unjustified, uncon-trolled and irresponsible power." To Drucker, this legitimacy crisis denied the large enterprise the necessary social sanction to serve as the integrating nucleus of the postwar industrial society. The crisis had to be ended for the new society to function.[60]

In the closing pages of *Management* Drucker declares the crisis over. "Almost three centuries ago," he begins, "the English pamphle-teer [Bernard] Mandeville in a didactic poem 'The Fable of the Bees' laid down what became a century later, the principle of capitalism, 'private vices make public benefits.'" The "invisible hand" of the market worked this miracle by transforming cupidity and greed into social virtues. However it may work economically, morally Mandeville's maxim is unacceptable. "And the fact that capitalism has become the less acceptable the more it succeeded—as the great Austro–American economist Joseph Schumpeter pointed out repeatedly—has been the basic weakness of modern society and modern economy."

Necessary to make capitalism acceptable is a principle of morality to justify the role of management in the society of organizations. "There is only one such principle. It is the purpose of organization and, therefore, the grounds of management authority: *to make human strength productive.*" The new maxim of justification to replace "private vices make public benefits" is "personal strengths make social benefits." Drucker's search for a moral basis for managerial authority is at an end. "This can serve as grounds for legitimacy. This is a moral principle on which authority can be based."[61]

In modernity the organization does more than accomplish all social tasks. It justifies the economic system. This elevated view would be tested in the years ahead as organizations began to turn on society by casting off tens of thousands of organization men and women.

# 7

# The Age of Discontinuity

FEW BOOKS of social analysis published in the 1960s still
speak to us today. What the historians call "presentism" binds them to
their urgent times, when lyric poems sought to save the country from
racism and war by the third stanza. Consider the cruel way time has
treated three of the biggest books of the decade. A best-seller in its day,
generously excerpted in the *New Yorker,* desperately "with it," *The
Greening of America* (1970), a hymn to the advanced consciousness of
the hippie, is now an embarrassment to nostalgia. *The New Industrial
State* (1967) by the economist John Kenneth Galbraith is a brilliant
book now unfortunately obsolete. History proved indifferent to one of
its central themes. Professor Galbraith depicted corporate management
as the vanguard of a new elite or "technostructure" whose power
could not be checked by supine stockholders or weak boards of directors. That was a fair approximation of truth at the time, yet within a
dozen years, to the applause of stockholders, raiders leading hostile
takeovers commenced to cashier professional managements everywhere. Michael Harrington's *The Other America* (1962) was the most
influential book on society of the decade, rightly credited with making
the poverty of 50 million Americans shamefully visible. But the causes
and consequences of poverty today are different from those depicted in
*The Other America,* dating its substance (not its moral witness) badly.

By contrast, from title to substance, Drucker's 1969 book, *The Age of Discontinuity*, reads as if written yesterday.

As a concept with which to make sense of contemporary thought and feeling, *The Age of Discontinuity* feels diagnostically right—it's got our number. Yet, while it all but ignores Vietnam, student protest, and the Civil Rights movement, *The Age of Discontinuity* is also a very 1960s book in its conviction that truth lies under the surface. Drucker will not accept the old list of problems and solutions as the sum of all such as themselves. There are realities beneath the official realities, trends under the trends. Drucker enlists geology to explain the novel purview of *The Age of Discontinuity:* "It attempts . . . to identify and to define changes that are occurring or have already occurred in the foundations. Its themes are the continental drifts that form new continents, rather than the wars that form new boundaries."[1]

These discontinuities are "major changes in the underlying social and cultural reality"; and these "rather than the massive momentum of the apparent trends are likely to mold and shape . . . the closing decades of the twentieth century." The discontinuities in technology, economy, government, and knowledge that Drucker identifies virtually define the American now. He had our future in his bones.[2]

The basic movement of Drucker's mind throughout his work is to contrast not only what is with what ought to be, but with what is thought to be. *The Age of Discontinuity* is built on that act of the critical imagination. Because Drucker is not in thrall to the basic assumptions of economics, he see realities to which economic theory denies the possibility of existence. He does not contest the truth of existing theory. He questions its adequacy. He does not develop new theory to fit the new realities. He shows the need for new theory. More than a quality of his voice, irony is the habit of his mind.

*     *     *

DRUCKER'S FIRST discontinuity is in industry and technology, and to understand it we have to see the twentieth century through his eyes. His world has a different history from the textbook's. He does not see new things but new connections among things long known; Drucker's past is as fresh and as unexpected as Drucker's futures. For example, we think of our century as a revolutionary time in industry and technology; Drucker demurs. Suppose, he asks us, an economist fell asleep the day he heard his father and Thomas Masaryk mourning the end of a world, waking only in 1968. Would he be surprised by the economic changes all around him? On the contrary, Drucker says, he would be surprised by how *little* things had changed. As if the two world wars had not happened, by the 1960s the industrial countries were reaching the levels of productivity and income that a 1914 economist would probably have predicted based on trends moored, thank you, in the *nineteenth* century. This is also true of technology. From the telephone to the automobile to the place of steel in urban civilization, the twentieth century largely lived off the technological innovation of the thirty years *before* 1914. That hangover from the nineteenth century lasted up until the 1960s, when time snapped, breaking the long continuity linking us to Edison, Marconi, and the Wright Brothers. "While we were busy finishing the great nineteenth-century economic edifice, the foundations have shifted under our feet." This shift in the foundations, and our corresponding sense of living on the near side of an historical divide, is the basic discontinuity of our times.[3]

"Four new industries are already in sight." The first is the information industry. Information, Drucker notes is "energy" for the mind, making this "the first era when energy for mind work has been available." The impact of cheap, reliable, and universally available information will rival the impact of electricity. "Certainly young people, a few years hence, will use information systems as their normal tools, much as they now use the typewriters and the telephone." Certainly.[4]

The second new industry, as yet still in prospect, is the rediscovery of the oceans as "the greatest economic resource to be found on earth." Within roughly the same generation 7,000 years ago the pyramids were built and the plow invented. "I suspect that space explorations are our 'pyramids' and the exploration of the oceans our 'plow.'"

"Materials" is the third new industry Drucker sees on the horizon of the 1960s. He regards plastics as "the only major industry that is rooted in twentieth-century rather than nineteenth-century science." Nature's materials over the millennia—paper, glass, steel, concrete, timber—will soon be augmented by more designer materials like plastic, completing a "shift from starting with what nature provides to what man wants to accomplish." That sentence reflects Drucker's humanism; man is ever his measure. He has no interest in technology for its own sake, and frequently criticizes technological hubris. For Drucker, technology is a bridge not a destination.[5]

"From what nature provides to what man wants to accomplish . . ." That sentence also suggests why Drucker's thought has a hopeful cast—especially in *The Age of Discontinuity.* Though it identifies and discusses "very serious problems," *The Age of Discontinuity* envisions them "as great opportunities for fresh thinking, policies, and for

---

### Four Marketing Lessons for the Future

—buying customers by underpricing boomerangs
—one can use market research only on what is already in the market
—the customer rather than the maker defines a market
—marketing starts with *all* customers in the market rather than with *our* customers.

—*Managing for the Future: The 1990's and Beyond* (1992)

a great outburst of creative energy in political thought and political action, in educational thought . . . and in economic thought."[6]

A whole set of new industries, fourth and finally, will arise from
megalopolis. People won't go to work, to take one example, work will
go to people. Well ahead of the reality that, as documented by *U.S.
News & World Report,* seven million people now telecommute at least
one day a week, Drucker sees no reason why knowledge workers can't
work at home. "[T]he great nineteenth-century achievement, the ability to move people," Drucker writes in a 1989 essay, "The Future's Already Around Us," has outlived its usefulness; witness the horrors of
daily commuting in most big cities and the smog that hovers over the
increasingly clogged traffic arteries." (To a business group wanting to
revitalize downtown Dallas by putting up office buildings, Drucker
once said, "What is the point of spending such huge sums to bring a
200-lb.-body downtown when all you want of it is its eight-and-a-
half-pound brain?") Only a mass transit system that provides general
access while also allowing for random movements "can solve the crisis
that threatens to paralyze megalopolis. . . ." That alternative transporta-
tion system whose boundary conditions—general access and random
movement—Drucker lays out would be among the major innovations
of the twenty-first century.[7]

Knowledge drives the new industries. "Knowledge, that is, systematic, purposeful, organized information had almost nothing to do with
the nineteenth-century innovations." They were experience-based;
the new industries are knowledge-based. They are not "additions" but
"innovations," and business and government must innovate to accom-
modate them.[8]

The commanding place of knowledge in the new economy, however, is not an unmitigated good. "Knowledge workers cannot be satisfied with work that is only a livelihood." Having tasted of the cup of
learning, the knowledge worker may early exhaust the stimulatory potential of his job; if not promoted or given an invigorating new chal-

lenge, he may retire on the job and suffer the curse of boredom until he collects his gold watch. The American workplace abounds in people too smart for their jobs. This unused capacity makes the job into a cage; it is also a drain on the economy. Redesigning work will not result in social benefit, however, if it ends in mass unemployment. Michael Hammer, the guru of reengineering who charges a reported $50,000 a day to tell companies how to save money, has been quoted as saying, "I don't think we've come close to squeezing out what's available to be squeezed out." Putting the whole economy through the neo-Taylorist wringer of reengineering, he estimates, could boost unofficial unemployment to 20 percent.[9]

The military handles the problem of job burnout by promoting officers out of the service, but this can be a civil rights violation outside the military. Hobbies are no answer: "Being an amateur does not satisfy a man who has learned to be a professional." A return to school for reskilling or renewal can be disappointing. "No allowance is made for the experience and knowledge of a mature man." Educators "see something morally wrong in not insisting on the 'required' two years of a course on business economics from the man who, in his working life, has proven himself an able economist. . . ." Finally, normal retirement at sixty-five years of age is no answer because it is "simply much too late a retirement age from the first occupation for the great majority of knowledge workers." If the knowledge worker simply retires without taking on new work "he is likely to disintegrate fast, knowledge work being habit forming in a way that manual work is not." So what's a restive knowledge worker to do?[10]

In a 1968 interview with *Psychology Today* that prompted seven hundred personal letters and hundreds of phone calls from people hungry for new work and challenge, Drucker said: "I am absolutely convinced that one of the greatest needs is the systematic creation of second careers." He added: "The older professions are best suited for second careers. Middle age is really the best time to switch to being the lawyer, the doctor, and the social worker." (In his later writings he tempers this breezy view; applying one's expertise to a new job in a new field becomes his recipe for renewal.) In the end the knowledge worker will simply have

> to learn that it is no disgrace in starting over again at age forty-five. . . . And he will have to learn that a second career at this age is a great deal more satisfying—and fun—than the bottle, a torrid affair with a chit of a girl . . . or any one of the customary attempts to mask one's frustration and boredom with work that, only a few years before, had been exciting, challenging, and satisfying.[11]

According to some writers on work, there is an intrinsic conflict between the organization's need to design work according to Taylorist dicta of efficiency and the human need to grow through new experience. If this view is correct, then the one sure way to reduce boredom in the workplace is to reduce the number of hours it must be endured. In *The End of Work,* Jeremy Rifkin reports that over the last thirty years or so annual work time has on average increased by 163 hours, while the average US worker has three-and-a-half fewer vacation and sick days. Over a quarter of US workers now put in more than forty-nine hours a week; as a result, leisure time has declined by a third. A shorter work week would give the incipiently bored knowledge worker more time to do more things that may matter to him more than work. Drucker might favor a shorter work week, but he would scorn this rea-

---

### On Fleas and Elephants

"Large organizations cannot be versatile. A large organization is effective through its mass rather than through its agility. Fleas can jump many times their own height, but not elephants."

—*The Age of Discontinuity* (1962)

soning. For him work is the arena of achievement. Leisure is "hob-bies."[12]

Theorists of *homo ludens* disagree. They see impersonal modern work as a fetter on the spirit. "Only perhaps in our Western industrial culture," David Riesman writes, "is work sharply set off against love, against pleasure, against consumption, against almost every sort of free-dom." What is needed is not more or different work; nearly everything eventually becomes routine, after all. It is a new social ideal: "freedom in play." Riesman again: "Far from having to be the residue sphere left over from work-time and work-feeling, [play] can increasingly become the sphere for the development of skill and competence in the art of living."[13]

Asked what he does in his leisure time, remember, Drucker an-swered, *What* leisure time? Asked to comment on the apparent irony of studying large organizations without ever working in one, he replied: "I couldn't work in a large organization. They bore me to tears." Does he suppose we can bear more boredom than he can? In any case he does not project that candid realism on work. Instead he projects his own prodigally creative experience of work. Biography is both source and limit of thought.[14]

THE CHANGES in technology and industry Drucker sees coming are immense and uncannily prescient. But they may be less wrenching than the second discontinuity to which he addresses him-self—the shift from an international to a world economy. This is such a major feature on our mental maps today that we need to remind our-selves that Drucker wrote in the late 1960s, when "made in Japan" still meant tinny goods.

The "international economy" introduced in eighteenth-century Europe and dominant worldwide from 1900, Drucker says, was based on separate national economies "with their own economic values and preferences, their own 'markets' and their own 'largely self-contained information.'" Adam Smith and David Ricardo established the principle of the international economy: comparative advantage. Since the climate of Portugal favors grapes, and the climate of England favors sheep grazing, it makes sense to exchange Portuguese wine for British wool. Trade naturally flows between economies that are "complementary" or produce different things like Portugal's and Britain's, not economies that are "competitive" or produce the same things like Britain's and America's.[15]

The new world economy stands that theory of trade on its head. "The more nearly equal two countries are in their economic structure, their technology, and their factorial costs," Drucker writes, "the greater and more intensive the trade between them." The key commodity in the world economy is knowledge, and it is much easier to transfer knowledge, whether in the shape of direct investment or through the migration of knowledge workers, "between areas of comparable knowledge level—that is, between countries on the same level of development—than it is to transfer knowledge where there are not many people ready to receive it." Of course complementary trade in region-dependent industries like farming and oil continues. But competitive trade based on knowledge is the dynamic of what Drucker calls the "global shopping center."[16]

"In an international economy there are no common appetites, no common demands." But in the world economy the pattern of demand, no longer confined by national economies, is worldwide. In an extraordinary passage Drucker explores this phenomenon.[17]

A universal appetite for small luxuries has emerged. They signify a little independence, a little control over economic destiny. They are a badge of freedom. Where the means are very limited—among the poor or among teenagers without much income of their own—the small luxury may be a soft drink, a lipstick, a movie magazine, or a candy bar. For the emerging middle class, it may be the appliance in the kitchen. For the truly affluent it may be an advanced academic degree. That one can do without it makes the small luxury into a psychological necessity.

That is the perception of a moralist operating on economic facts. The insight is not into trade but into manners and the human psyche. With Drucker, economics returns to its roots in moral philosophy.

"The world economy is not yet a community—not even an economic community," he writes, and the years since bear that out. "Yet the existence of the 'global shopping center' is a fact that cannot be undone. The vision of an economy for all will not be forgotten again." An economy for all: that is the grail of globalism.[18]

DRUCKER'S LAST "discontinuity" is "disenchantment with government." His administration, President Nixon pledged, would prove Peter Drucker wrong; it would show that government can succeed in more than inflating the currency and waging war. In the event, the Nixon administration inflated the currency and waged war. This only deepened the emerging disenchantment with government. Watergate deepened it further. The nation was heading for a rendezvous with Ronald Reagan who, in his 1981 inaugural address, said "Government is not the solution: Government is the problem."

By contrast, "The generations that reached manhood between 1918 and 1960," Drucker says, were "in love" with government. What happened? And what can be done to close a breach between people and government that travesties the democratic idea of self-rule?[19]

In his chapter on "The Sickness of Government" Drucker points the way to answers that remain fresh today. "What explains this disenchantment with government?" he asks; and answers, "We expected miracles—and that always produces disillusionment."[20]

But was it the expectation of miracles or specific government actions that brought on the disenchantment? According to a recent paper by the Kennedy School of Government's Gary Orren, public trust in government fell by 15 points between 1964 and 1968, the years of U.S. escalation in Vietnam; by another 8 points during President Nixon's first two years; and by another 17 points in the wake of Watergate and President Ford's pardoning of Nixon. In short, malperformance and the brazen abuse of power, not thaumaturgic expectations, drove the crisis of confidence in government. With his honed eye for the trend, Drucker identified a problem with a future, but missed its source.

Drucker will have none of the conservative doctrine that the weaker government the better; the complex responsibilities that modern society and economy have thrust upon government at all levels cannot be evaded. In the spirit of Vice President Al Gore's "performance review" of the federal government, which begins, "The federal government is not simply broke; it is broken," Drucker wants to fix government, not tear it down to clear the field for Darwinian capitalism. Never, he writes, "has strong, effective, truly performing government been needed more than in this dangerous world of ours." Government is not simply a drain on the economy: "Effective government is a prerequisite of social and economic growth."[21]

With nuanced argument, Drucker defends government against Rotarian cliche. Yes, government resists change, but its "inability to innovate is grounded in government's legitimate and necessary function as society's protective and conserving organ." Yes, government is a poor manager, but "government is also properly conscious of the fact that it administers public funds and must account for every penny. It has no choice but to be bureaucratic. . . . Any government that is not a 'government of forms' degenerates rapidly into a mutual looting society." Government would manage better if it were not so directly responsive to politics, which, "rightly," focuses on "new" "hot" programs, crises, issues and not "on doing a job." Government would work better, in fine, if there were none or fewer of those disturbers of the bureaucratic peace—elections. This is by way of being a classic answer to the conservative question: Why can't government be run like a business?[22]

The defining characteristics of government make it a poor "doer," too liable to politically inspired inefficiencies. "The purpose of government is to make fundamental decisions . . . to focus the political energies of society . . . to dramatize issues . . . to present fundamental choices"—not to operate bureaucracies. Industry separates "decision making organs from doing." "In business this goes by the name of 'decentralization.' . . . The purpose is to make it possible for top management to concentrate on decision" by leaving "doing to operating managements." Why, Drucker asks, can't government work the same way? Set broad policy, supply the funding, and leave social tasks to the "new nongovernmental institutions that have sprung up and grown these last sixty to seventy years." With its linkup to private colleges and universities the GI Bill after World War II is an especially popular example of what Drucker has in mind. It created a new model "through which the government would *regulate* and *provide* but not do," the historian Michael J. Bennett writes in his 1993 book on the GI Bill, *When Dreams Came True,* which cites Drucker on the meaning and model of the GI Bill.[23]

Drucker calls this social innovation "reprivatization." It would assign to business and nonprofit organizations the "tasks which flowed to government in the last century because the original private institution of society, the family, could not discharge them. . . ." Reprivatization, shorn of its prefix, is perhaps Drucker's most frequently invoked concept.

It is likely to be the budgetary nostrum of twenty-first-century public finance, to judge by the late-nineties calls for privatizing everything from highway maintenance to the Internal Revenue Service.

Tony Blair, the first Labour prime minister of Britain in twenty years, speaks for politicians on the left and right who see a future in which "the role of government is not necessarily to provide all social provision, but to organize and regulate it"—what Drucker was saying thirty years ago. As with outsourcing, privatization recommends itself to Drucker on grounds broader than efficiency. The parceling out of tasks once performed by big public bureaucracies to smaller private entities creates new opportunities for employee advancement as the civic service principle of seniority in promotion and job preference yields to the business principle of performance. Drucker served as a consultant to the Pentagon through the Kennedy–Johnson years, an experience that left him with vivid convictions about the evils of bureaucracy.

Business would be an especially appropriate doer of social tasks because "of all institutions, it is the only one created for the express purpose of making and managing change." Also, "alone among all institutions," business has a test of performance—profitability (a test dubiously applicable to the performance of social tasks)."[24]

The trouble with Drucker's bold reinvention of government— with the civic logic of privatization—is that it elides the cardinal difference between government and business or nonprofit organizations—democratic accountability. Lumbering, swollen, seemingly impervious to opinion, influence, and appeal, government *in principle* is still answerable to the people. That is not true of business nor even of nonprofit organizations. Drucker's scheme would trade democratic consent and scrutiny for social innovation. That would be a mixed bargain even if the social innovation worked because it would subordinate the citizen to the customer or the client.

Moreover, as millions of Americans under "managed care" medical plans can testify, for-profit privatization of social goods like health care can mean less, not more, choice. HMO's couldn't save money, the claim made for the nonprofits, much less make a profit if they let patients choose their doctors. Privatization understood as profitization can mean more economic freedom for private organizations but less economic freedom for individuals.

Drucker is undoubtedly right when he says that "we will need new political theory and probably very new constitutional law" to think through, much less to implement, the whole project of privatization. For him privatization is not an ideological totem based on the puerile dichotomy that "public" is bad and "private" is good. Privatization is a means toward the end of restoring confidence not in a government that "does" or "administers" but in "a government that governs." As such, privatization should perhaps not be contrasted with "government-run," but rather with other proposals for restoring confidence in government like campaign finance reform, term limits, national referenda and recall, a constitutional amendment striking down the 1976 Supreme Court decision that money equals speech, laws making election day a national holiday, and laws requiring television networks and stations to donate time for the candidates to run ads or make speeches—lots of time. Compared to these narrowly focused political steps to mitigate political alienation, privatization looks like the solution to a different problem.[25]

SPEAKING OF "strong, effective, truly performing government," Drucker says, "Never has it been needed more than in the present world economy." Government must be strong enough "in the international sphere so that we can make the sacrifices of sovereignty needed to give us working supranational institutions for world society and world economy." These are the very terms of the 1993–94 debate in Congress over U.S. entry into the World Trade Organization. Drucker was his customary thirty years ahead of events.[26]

The new world economy and the disenchantment with government make a dangerous combination. The world economy causes the most wrenching of the changes involved in Drucker's discontinuities because it affects the livelihoods and lives of millions. The disenchantment with government will hurt our ability to compete in the new economy. "Until we recognize that global competition has as much to do with the quality of our government as it does with the efficiency of our corporations," Derek Bok writes, in words Drucker would strongly endorse, "we are likely to continue lagging behind other democracies in pursuing the goals that matter most." What should government do to protect lives and livings? Or, to use Drucker's standard of effectiveness, what *can* government do?

Drucker recommends a dramatic reorientation of education away from an almost exclusive concentration on "extended learning" for young people to a new emphasis on "continuous learning" for adults. Even though "The academic community is still somewhat suspicious of anyone past adolescence who wants to learn," Drucker writes, "when knowledge is applied to work, we need . . . the frequent return of the experienced and accomplished adult to formal learning." Continuous learning would be an innovative public sector response to the exposure of the American workforce to a world economy in which knowledge is our comparative advantage. And there is also an open field here for entrepreneurship on the GI Bill model. "I think the growth industry of the future," Drucker told an interviewer in 1994, "in this country and the world will soon be the continuing education of adults. Nothing else is growing as fast. . . . I think the educated person of the future is somebody who realizes the need to continue to learn. That is the new definition and it is going to change the world we live in and work in."[27]

Extended learning is something we should rethink not only for the sake of economics but for the sake of equality of opportunity. "Limiting access to opportunity to those with a diploma is a crass denial of all fundamental beliefs—beliefs, by the way, that have been amply validated by experience." Making the professor the gatekeeper of social hope "restricts, oppresses, and injures individual and society alike." Drucker looks forward to the day when state legislatures will sponsor referenda to ban questions in employment applications about "educational status," just as laws already ban questions about the applicant's race. "I, for one, shall vote for this proposal if I can," he says, academic ability, like race, "is also an accident of birth, and not a very meaningful one at that." From *Industrial Man* to *The Age of Discontinuity*, Drucker insists that major social institutions must not contradict the basic beliefs of a society—which is why, for fifty years, he has sought to change the authoritarian workplace and the inequality-ratifying school.[28]

One step Drucker does not want government to take is to resort to protectionism or subsidy to preserve jobs. "A country, an industry, or a company that puts the preservation of blue-collar manufacturing jobs ahead of being internationally competitive (and that implies steady shrinkage of such jobs)," he writes in "The Changed World Economy," a major essay from the 1980s, "will soon have neither production nor steady jobs. . . . [A] country will have the less *general* unemployment the faster it shrinks blue-collar employment in manufacturing." Take Britain: behind its trading partners in cutting manufacturing jobs, it paid the price in high general unemployment in the 1970s and 1980s. In his debate with Karl Polanyi, Drucker could cite Britain as an example of the often perverse consequences of policies seeking to protect society from economic change.

"We may well conclude that the new reality means we can no longer control the economic 'weather' of recession and boom cycles, unemployment, savings and spending rates." Drucker says in a 1989 interview, making another of his conceptual distinctions, "but only the 'climate'—avoiding protectionism, or educating the working population to function in a knowledge society. In short, preventive medicine instead of blind attempts at short-term fixes."[29]

Of course without "supranational organizations" to bring a measure of stability to the world economy, reinventing education and avoiding protectionism will not by themselves ensure prosperity. To keep the transition from the local economies of the nineteenth century to the national economy of the twentieth from leaving millions of Americans behind took incremental governmental innovation from the Progressive Era to the New Deal. Economist Robert Borosage describes the progressive response to the national economy: "The Industrial Revolution produced a national market dominated by great corporate trusts. . . . Progressives, led by [Theodore] Roosevelt, forged a bi-partisan coalition to put boundaries around the market. Against fierce resistance of the most purblind corporations . . . Progressives fought for anti-trust laws, food and drug regulation, child labor bans, a minimum wage and a progressive income tax. Roosevelt's 'New Nationalism' laid the groundwork for 20th century economic reforms and the creation of the great American middle class." Now the national economy is being eclipsed by the world economy, but the disenchantment with government, fed and furthered by powerful interests, won't even permit debate over governmental innovations, domestic and supranational, to assure a broad prosperity and to balance growth with security. That is why our loss of confidence in government, which has sunk to depths Drucker could not imagine in 1968, remains as Drucker called it, "the most profound discontinuity" of our times.

An allied discontinuity that Drucker discusses in his later work, notably in *The New Realities* (1989), is the break between yesterday's amalgamating politics of economic interests—the Republican coalition put together in 1896 by Mark Hanna and the Democratic coalition put together in 1932 by Franklin D. Roosevelt—and today's divisive "single interest pluralism." In his 1994 *Atlantic Monthly* essay Drucker writes: "Increasingly, politics is not about 'who gets what, when, how' but about values, each of them considered to be absolute. Politics is about 'the right to life' . . . It is about the environment. It is about gaining equality for groups alleged to be oppressed . . . None of these issues is economic. All are fundamentally moral." Economic interests can be compromised. "'Half a loaf is still bread' is a meaningful saying. . . . To an environmentalist 'half an endangered species' is an extinct species."[30]

In this new politics "so far there is no political concept, no political integration" that fits the knowledge worker, who remains up for grabs electorally. In *The New Realities* Drucker outlines the difficulty of bringing the knowledge worker into a new political integration along Hanna/Roosevelt lines:

> Knowledge workers are neither farmers nor labor nor business; they are employees of organizations. Yet they are not "proletarians" and do not feel "exploited" as a class. Collectively, [as we will see] they are the only "capitalists" through their pension funds. Many of them are themselves "bosses" and have subordinates. Yet they also have a boss themselves. They are not middle class, either. They are, to coin a term "uniclass . . ."

This is not a description of the archetypal Democrat or Republican. In 1992 Ross Perot captured 20 percent of the vote by appealing primarily to knowledge workers. In 1996 they strongly backed Bill Clinton. Knowledge workers, not the blue-collar "Reagan Democrats" of the 1980s, are the new swing vote in American politics. And, in order to feel at home in either major party, they may have to force reform of today's investor-driven politics.

IN *The New Society* Drucker presented his vision of an industrial community in which the relations between worker and management would be founded on an identity of interest in the prosperity of the enterprise. The year the book appeared, 1950, Drucker worked closely with Charles Wilson, GM president, to develop a pension plan for GM workers that both men saw as a route to industrial community. Drucker tells the story of what happened to their vision in *The Unseen Revolution: How Pension Fund Socialism Came to America* (1976), since retitled *The Pension Fund Revolution.*

A pension plan tied to the economic performance of GM, both Wilson and Drucker hoped, would establish a "community of interest" between workers and management. What was good for GM would be good for its pensioners. Also, the pension would tend to inhibit union militancy, a major obstacle to industrial community. Inflicting a long strike on a company on which retirees depended for their pensions could split the union's own community of interest between retired and active members. Drucker would have disavowed any antiunion intention, but the effect of the pension was to create an unmeditated bond between worker and management. "One of the stalwarts in the GM department of the UAW," he writes in *The Pension Fund Revolution,* "proposed at the time, in all seriousness, that the union should lodge an unfair labor practices complaint against Wilson, since his pension proposal could have no purpose except to undermine the union."[31]

In the event, as we will see, the kind of pension plan GM chose, and most other large corporations quickly emulated, had baneful economy-wide consequences *and* also failed to create a community of interest. The employee came to regard a pension fund whose managers were "appointed by and accountable only to company management" as the "company's fund." "The employees do not feel that it makes any difference how the fund performs," Drucker wrote in 1986, when the unambiguous results were in. "And they are right: Unless the company goes bankrupt it does not make a difference to them." Another

Drucker attempt to create a model of industrial community had failed.[32]

There remained one more option in Drucker's quest: to break down the wall separating labor and management by bringing labor *into* management. As we have seen, Drucker rejected this step in 1950 as an economically risky burden on management. *The Pension Fund Revolution* shows no change in this view. By the 1980s, however, it had changed. In 1982 three different union leaders came, separately, to seek Drucker's counsel. All three were worried that unions were courting irrelevancy. To illustrate, one of them described the conflict between the economic imperatives of the new world economy and the political realities of unions. "It is our proudest boast that the total wage package in our industry is some 30 percent to 40 percent higher than the average wage package in American manufacturing," this union leader said. "But would there be record unemployment in our industry . . . if that 30 percent to 40 percent had been put into plant modernization instead of into wages and benefits? I know that all my colleagues in the union leadership ask themselves this question. But no one dares come out with it in the open—he wouldn't last ten minutes if he did." Fearful of the charge of "selling out to management," union leaders dared not confront their members with such issues as capital formation (to invest in modernization) and productivity growth (to afford high wages). To focus on these things, Drucker writes, "would be tantamount to accepting that the interests of the enterprise and the interests of its employees are identical—and this would be seen as a denial of the union's very reason for existence."[33]

In "Are Labor Unions Becoming Irrelevant?," a *Wall Street Journal* essay, Drucker writes that only through what the Germans call "codetermination" could workers be brought to see what their leaders see: that in the world economy labor must display new flexibility on wages and benefits to keep tomorrow's jobs in the US. By joining management the unions could grapple directly with the forces threatening their jobs—foremost among them, corporate mobility in an age of portable technology and open markets, but also including executive salaries and stockholder dividends and insufficient investment in new plants and equipment. Drucker does not want unions to become irrelevant. "Modern society, a society of organizations each requiring strong management, needs an organ such as the labor union—events in Poland" [referring to the role played by Solidarity in the protest against the communist authorities] "have amply proved this." But unless unions can reconcile the conflict between the new economy and their candor-averse politics, he fears the worst. That conflict is another face of the dichotomy between growth and security. To preserve security in the world economy the labor movement must change its old economy focus on one country. In a major social innovation of the sort Drucker feels is necessary, labor must become as global as capital. The universalist vision of democratic socialism that was destroyed in 1914 has a new lease on relevance. To save the local community from being submerged by the emerging national economy of the late nineteenth century, reformers realized that they had to win control of the national state. So the labor movement today has no choice but to organize globally to defend what it has won nationally.[34]

ONLY THOSE who regularly use terms like "annuities" will enjoy *The Pension Fund Revolution,* at once Drucker's most provocative and dullest book, though even Shakespeare might fail before the subject of pensions. Reduced to one sentence, his thesis is that, since they hold most of the equity of American business, employee pension plans are today's capitalists. The "owners" of big business are the workers employed by big business.

*The Pension Fund* begins with one of Drucker's attention-riveting first sentences: "If 'socialism' is defined as 'ownership of the means of

production'—and this is both the orthodox and the only rigorous definition—then the United States is the first truly 'Socialist' country."
Drucker's interest had been drawn to the pension fund phenomenon
by several of his former students at New York University who, as early
as 1960, founded a brokerage, Donaldson, Lufkin & Jenrette, to cater
exclusively to pension funds. Fourteen years later pension funds were
the leading institutional investors on Wall Street. Through these funds
America's employees owned 25 percent of business equity capital (re-
visiting the subject 15 years later, Drucker found the percentage had
grown to 40 percent). "The means of production, that is, the American economy—is being run for the benefit of the country's employees.
Profits increasingly become retirement pensions, that is, 'deferred
compensation' of the employees."[35]

To be sure, many workers were excluded from this new *rentier* class
of employee-owners. By Drucker's estimate, only 50 million of the 85
to 90 million employees in the U.S. work force in 1973 participated in
pension funds. And fully a tenth of Americans reaching retirement age
would receive "no benefits at all." Pension-fund socialism generated
nearly as much inequality as old-fashioned capitalism.[36]

The founder of American Socialism was Charles Wilson; his instrument was the GM pension fund. Earlier pension funds had been
"annuity" plans, to be invested in standard life insurance investments
such as government bonds. Wilson's "major innovation was a pension
fund investing in the 'American economy'—in other words, the free-
enterprise system."

The rise of pension fund socialism reflected a dramatic change in
the demographics of old age. People born in the 1890s were living on
into the 1960s and 1970s. The demographic revolution of the last
seventy years had created a huge constituency of the retired and the
middle-aged "for whom pensions are a major concern. . . ."

One of Drucker's favorite article titles is "The Problem of Success." It encapsulates the rounded wisdom of his mature point of view. Drucker outlines several "problems of success" facing pension funds. Here are two:

- Increasingly older and younger workers will have different interests in union/management negotiations, with the former pressing for an increase in pensions, the latter for an increase in wages. "Equally, there is a built-in tension between the people at work and earning, and the needs of retired ex-workers on pension."
- Control of the capital market is shifting from "entrepreneurs" to the "trustees, from the people who are supposed to invest in the future to the people who have to follow 'the prudent man rule,' which means, in effect investing in past performance." Would pension-fund managers slow economic growth by an excess of prudence in investing?

UNLIKE THE real thing, pension fund socialism has "had very little impact on American institutions, American power structure, American politics, even on American political rhetoric. . . . As far as its impact upon the system is concerned, pension fund socialism can only be called trivial." This is largely because pension fund socialism comes twinned with finance capitalism—"if by 'capitalism' is meant resource allocation in and through a market mechanism." This feature explains why pension-fund socialism has had trivial effects on the economic, social, and political status quo—because it is really pension-fund capitalism. Capitalist values, not socialist values, dictate the investment choices of the pension-fund managers who are bound by fiduciary duty to invest in only the most profitable, not in the most socially responsible, companies. The identity of the pensioners does not matter;

they could be corporate executives or socialist college professors. The funds would act in the same way: to reap maximum returns for their principals.[37]

In a long review of *The Unseen Revolution* in the *New York Review of Books,* Jason Epstein argued that "pension-fund socialism" was essentially a Druckerian conceit. "Much of Drucker's disingenuousness in this book can be understood as the sort of torpid whimsy that high-priced business consultants concoct to amuse their clients—in the present case an exercise in late Hapsburg black humor, Drucker being a relic of that quaint epoch." In fact, Drucker does sustain the thesis of socialism by sportive Jesuitical argument, applying Marx's definitions of "means of production" and the like to the pension-fund phenomenon to ingenious but increasingly implausible effect. It is socialism on the page, an arid and mechanical proof. The search for industrial community had come down to mere words.[38]

The merit of *The Pension Fund Revolution* was to draw attention to the anomaly of an immense concentration of wealth that had not yet exerted power over the economy. In the 1980s pension funds would begin to exert their power—with effects that would shake the proud tower of management to its foundations.

# 8

# Bring Your Own Machete

IN THE spring of 1950 General Motors and the United Auto Workers (UAW) reached agreement on the country's largest private-sector pension fund; ruinous consequences have since flowed from the terms of that agreement. Drucker's friend and client (Drucker helped GM think through the pension issue), Charles Wilson and the UAW president, Walter Reuther, wanted a "defined contributions" benefits plan. Under it GM would pay a fixed annual sum into the plan and the retiree would receive either a fixed annual stipend or a sum that would vary with the fund's earnings. GM's finance committee overruled Wilson, opting for a "defined benefits" plan. Under it the company would pay the retiree a fixed portion of his last salary, while its own contribution would go down if the fund's earnings went up and up if the earnings went down. GM counted on the stock market not to go down; as Drucker could have told GM, this was unwise. The variability of GM's contribution to the plan guaranteed constant company pressure on the fund managers to perform consistently well in the stock market.[1]

The GM/UAW agreement set the national pattern for pensions. "Within one year after its inception," Drucker writes in *The Pension Fund Revolution,* "8000 new plans had been written—four times as many as had been set up in the 100 years before—" with most modeled on GM's plan. The same agreement also set in train a crisis so grave that it threatened what Drucker called the "survival of the free-enterprise system."

The crisis began in 1980 with the first wave of "hostile takeovers" of major corporations. In "The Hostile Takeover and Its Discontents," a lucid explanation of the whole phenomenon published in the *Public Interest* in 1986, Drucker calculated the number of takeovers as between four and five hundred—"with at least one half ending in the disappearance of the target company. . . ." (A recent estimate from a management textbook: "Between 1980 and 1987, 20 percent of all manufacturing assets changed hands in some form of financial transaction.")[2]

In a typical scenario, after buying some of the target company's stock, a "raider" offers to buy the company; management and the Board of Directors, as he expects, reject his offer. The raider then borrows banks' worth of money (often running to a billion or more dollars) to buy up something approaching a controlling quantity of the target company's available stock. To achieve the control that is now within his grasp, the raider offers to pay the company's other shareholders, pension funds usually representing the largest bloc, "substantially more than the current share price on the stock exchange" for their shares. If enough stockholders take what amounts to a bribe, the raider captures the company and quickly unloads on it the debt he incurred in the takeover. "In the hostile takeover," Drucker writes, invigorating a bloodless subject, "the victim thus ends up paying for his own execution."[3]

The pension funds play the role of executioner. "Without the concentration of voting power in a few pension funds," Drucker wrote in a 1991 article in the *Harvard Business Review,* ". . . most of the raiders' attacks would never have been launched." For the pension funds, failure to show market-leading if not market-breaking gains in their port-

folios can force the companies they represent to dip into current accounts to cover their defined-benefits contribution—thus paying for
yesterday with capital needed to invest in tomorrow. To prevent this financial regression the pension-fund managers must show short-term
gains *even* if this means siding with a raider. "Pension-fund managers
know that the raider's bid is deleterious to the company whose stock
they own," Drucker writes in a passage echoing Marx's mordant comment that "the capitalist is capital personified."

> But they cannot consider the welfare and interests of their "property."
> They are not owners. They are of necessity speculators, even though they
> are legally vested with the owner's power. And so they behave as specula-
> tors. They have to accept the raider's bid unless a white knight makes a
> better offer.[4]

Fearful of raiders, companies began practicing defensive capitalism.
"More and more of our businesses, large, medium-size, and small, are
not being run for business results but for protection against the hostile
takeover." Cutting spending on research and development, squander-
ing money to deny the raider the bait of cash-in-hand, managers were
running businesses for short-term results, letting "the future go hang."
Among both managers and professionals, "The fear of the raider de-
moralizes and paralyzes . . . 'What's the point in my trying to do a
good job if the rug will be pulled out from under me tomorrow?' is a
frequent comment." The human organization of the enterprise was
everywhere impaired as employees began to see themselves as "'chattel'
to be sold to the highest bidder."[5]

Any institution, Drucker notes in *Post-Capitalist Society,* "degenerates into mediocrity and malperformance if it is not clearly accountable to someone for results. This is what happened to the big American
corporation in the thirty years between 1950 and 1980." So long
wielding "unfounded, unjustified, uncontrolled and irresponsible

power," management was paying for years of ignoring stockholders and boards of directors (Galbraith was right about the immediate past) who betrayed managements just as soon as the price was right. Corporate capitalism—"that is, autonomous management, accountable to no one, controlled by no one, and without constituents—" was being humbled, disgraced, scorned.[6]

"What has hurt particularly," Drucker wrote in a 1988 piece for *Industry Week,* "are the 'golden parachutes' that make top management people rich in a hostile takeover or leveraged buyout while their middle management associates lose their jobs. . . ."

> But what hurts the most is that the new masters of American business (at least as perceived by middle managers and professionals)—the raiders, the junk-bond underwriters, the arbitrageurs and stock-exchange players—are so openly contemptuous of management people, of their focus on work rather than "deals," of their working for a salary rather than to become rich, and especially of their belief in the company as something of value in itself, as something to be proud of, as something to "belong" to.[7]

The institution of management, ensnared in the cash nexus, was being undermined. And social predators were bleeding fortunes from the wreck of great companies. The price of unrestricted economic freedom (abroad, takeovers were carefully regulated by government)

---

### On Overage Executives

"The basic rule, and one that should be clearly established, is that people beyond their early sixties should ease out of major managerial responsibilities. It is a sensible rule for anyone, and not only the executive, to stay out of decisions if one won't be around to help bail out the company when the decisions cause trouble a few years down the road—as most of them do."

—*The Frontiers of Management* (1986)

was rising. Economic motives, contrary to Drucker's anthropology, seemed to be the only motives that counted. "The hostile takeover bid," Drucker wrote with sadness, "is . . . the final failure of corporate capitalism."[8]

THIS WAS the context of Drucker's new focus on entrepreneurial capitalism and the nonprofit organization in the 1980s. For Drucker "the emergence of a truly entrepreneurial economy in the United States during the last ten or fifteen years [is] the most significant event to have occurred in recent economic and social history."[9]

He decided to write a book that would do for innovation and entrepreneurship what *Practice of Management* had done for management—make a discipline out of it by explaining its principles and practices. Once again, his timing was felicitous.[10]

Between 1965 and 1985, by Drucker's methodical reckoning, the U.S. economy created nearly 40 million jobs, while Europe was losing jobs, and Japan creating them at only half the U.S. rate. The new jobs were not coming from *Fortune* 500 companies, who were shedding jobs. They were not coming from government, universities, or hospitals. They were coming from small and medium-sized business; *The Economist* estimated that 600,000 new businesses were being started in the U.S. every year. *Innovation and Entrepreneurship,* published at the top of the jobs boom in 1985, sought to tutor this exuberance of new ventures.[11]

As Drucker saw it, a *social* technology was leveraging the boom: management. For most of the period since World War I management had attached to big business and its *managerial* side was emphasized, not its entrepreneurial side. "It was a period of high technological and entrepreneurial continuity," Drucker writes, "a period that required adaptation rather than innovation, and the ability to do better rather than the courage to do differently." In the entrepreneurial 1970s and

1980s management broke out of its corporate captivity. Like a new technology undergoing pervasive diffusion, it was applied to new enterprises, to small enterprises, to nonbusinesses, to "activities that were simply not considered to be enterprises at all, like local restaurants," and to systematic innovation itself. McDonald's is Drucker's classic example. No new technology; instead, the innovation was applying management concepts to the local hamburger stand.[12]

On the publication of *Innovation and Entrepreneurship* an interviewer for *Inc.* magazine asked Drucker if he agreed with the "conventional wisdom" that "there are managers and there are entrepreneurs, but that the two are not the same?" Yes and no, Drucker replied. "You see, there is entrepreneurial work and there is managerial work. But you can't be a successful entrepreneur unless you manage, and if you try to manage without some entrepreneurship, you are in danger of becoming a bureaucrat." Conceding that the conventional wisdom was right—that "managers" and "entrepreneurs" were antitypes in the sociology of appearances—would invite unwelcome reflection on the

---

### The Entrepreneur Returns

"Now we are entering again an era in which emphasis will be on entrepreneurship. However, it will not be the entrepreneurship of a century ago, that is, the ability of a single man to organize a business he himself could run, control, embrace. It will rather be the ability to create and direct an organization for the new. We need men who can build a new structure of entrepreneurship on the managerial foundations laid these last fifty years. History, it has often been observed, moves in a spiral; one returns to the preceding position, or to the preceding problem, but on a higher level, and by a corkscrew-like path. In this fashion we are going to return to entrepreneurship on a path that led out from a lower level, that of the single entrepreneur, to the manager, and now back, though upward, to entrepreneurship again."

—*The Age of Discontinuity* (1969)

image of the manager as a gray slave to the existing, and that of the entrepreneur as a creative bearer of the new. The entrepreneur is the folk hero of capitalism and Drucker wanted some of his prestige to rub off on the manager, who just then needed it badly. It was a portent that Drucker himself, the inventor of management, was growing uncomfortable "with the word *manager* . . . I find myself using executive more, because it implies responsibility for an area, not necessarily dominion over people."

Drucker was insensible to the romance of the entrepreneur. "The popular picture of innovators—half pop psychology, half Hollywood—makes them look like a cross between Superman and the Knights of the Round Table. Alas, most of them in real life are unromantic figures, and much more likely to spend hours on a cash-flow projection than to dash off in search of 'risk.'" There was no magic to entrepreneurship, a teachable discipline like chess. Not romance but biographical circumstance made entrepreneurship congenial to Drucker; the economics of innovation had been established by his father's friend and former colleague from the economics faculty of the University of Vienna, Joseph Schumpeter.[13]

IN A 1983 essay in *Forbes,* "Schumpeter and Keynes," Drucker contrasted the economics of the "two greatest economists of this century." Both were born in 1883: Schumpeter in a small Austrian town, Keynes in Cambridge, England. In the year of their centenary, Keynes, "with a host of books, articles, conferences, and speeches" in his honor, was the cynosure of all interest. "If the centenary of Schumpeter's birth were noticed at all," Drucker wrote, "it would be in a small doctoral seminar. And yet it is Schumpeter who will shape the thinking and inform the questions of economic theory and economic policy for the rest of this century, if not for the next thirty or fifty years."[14]

Drucker pictures Keynes as a "heretic" from classical economics whose key question, "How can one maintain an economy in balance and in stasis?" showed his underlying fealty to the "equilibrium economics of David Ricardo's 1810 theories." By contrast, Schumpeter was an "infidel" from the neoclassical economics of his teachers in the so-called Austrian school of economics. And for Schumpeter, Keynes asked the wrong question. "To him the basic fallacy was the very assumption that the healthy, 'normal,' economy is an economy in static equilibrium." Instead, incessantly churning, shifting, with some industries failing and others surging, the modern economy is in a state of "dynamic disequilibrium."[15]

To Keynes, to classical economics generally, in Drucker's telling, innovation belonged in the category of "outside catastrophes" like wars and earthquakes that influenced the economy, sometimes profoundly, but were too altogether incalculable as phenomena to belong to economics. To Schumpeter, "innovation—that is, entrepreneurship that moves resources from the old and obsolescent to new and more productive employments—is the very essence of economics and most certainly of a modern economy."[16]

If the hero of Keynes' economics is modernity's philosopher-king—the government economist working the levers of money, credit, spending, and demand in the *agon* of maintaining equilibrium—Schumpeter's hero is the entrepreneur venturing forth on a sea of risk swept by gales of "creative destruction," Schumpeter's famous phrase for the anarchic energy of innovation. Keynes was the prophet of the postwar economy, with its "high technological and entrepreneurial continuity." Schumpeter is the prophet of the age of discontinuity. He speaks to the "profound shift" going on around us from a "managerial" to an "entrepreneurial" economy, a distinction that, in this broad context, Drucker accepts.

It was Schumpeter's entrepreneur who breasted the formidable Kondratieff wave in the great jobs boom of 1965–1985, saving the U.S. economy from stagnation. A Russian economist killed by Stalin for (accurately) predicting that the collectivization of agriculture would return hunger to Russia, Nikolai Kondratieff theorized that the most basic forces in economic life are fifty-year waves of technological innovation followed by periods of stagnation. "Every fifty years . . . a long technological wave crested," Drucker writes in *Innovation and Entrepreneurship*. "For the last twenty years of this cycle, the growth industries of the last technological advance seem to be doing exceptionally well." But they are really living in the hectic afterglow of yesterday's technology. When the true state of things is revealed and industries begin to contract, the economy enters a twenty-year period of stagnation awaiting the still-nascent technology that will drive the next wave forward, but that is unable to create enough jobs to do so.

Applying this model to the postwar era, Drucker sees the major industries—"automobiles, steel, rubber, electrical apparatus, consumer electronics, telephones, but also petroleum—" as resting on nineteenth-century breakthroughs in technology, as he argued in *The Age of Discontinuity*. Apparently thriving through the 1960s, in fact they were "corroding from within" and beginning to suffer permanent job losses. Meanwhile, the emerging high-tech industries could not yet

---

### On Risk

"Of course innovation is risky. But so is stepping into the car to drive to the supermarket for a loaf of bread. All economic activity is by definition 'high risk.' And defending yesterday—that is, not innovating—is far more risky than making tomorrow."

—*Innovation and Entrepreneurship* (1985)

create the jobs to break the "stagflation" of the years after the 1973 oil shock. "Of the 40-million plus jobs created since 1965," Drucker writes, "high technology did not create more than five or six million." The new jobs that disturbed the trough in the Kondratieff wave came from the wholly unanticipated surge in entrepreneurialism led by the social innovation of bringing management to small enterprise. As a theory to describe the behavior of the American economy over the period 1965–1985, "Kondratieff can be considered disproven and discredited"—by the entrepreneur.[17]

The essence of entrepreneurship is "doing something different rather than doing better what already is being done." An entrepreneur innovates. "Innovation is the specific instrument of entrepreneurship. It is the act that endows resources with a new capacity to create wealth." Often spoken of as a change in technology, innovation "is an economic or social rather than a technical term." Using familiar and esoteric examples from business history, Drucker devotes sections and chapters to the "seven sources of innovative opportunity," "the principles of innovation," "the bright idea," "the new venture," and a jaunty pair of entrepreneurial strategies for established firms, "Fustest with the Mostest," and "Hit Them Where They Ain't." He also discusses "the entrepreneurial business," rejecting by example (Johnson & Johnson, 3M) and argument the notion that big business, stopped by "the

---

### The Innovative Company

"Ideas are somewhat like babies—they are born small, immature, and shapeless. They are promise rather than fulfillment. In the innovative company executives do not say, 'This is a damn-fool idea.' Instead they ask, 'What would be needed to make this embryonic, half-baked, foolish idea into something that makes sense, that is an opportunity for us?'"

—*The Frontiers of Management* (1986)

obstacle of the existing," cannot innovate. To overcome that obstacle, he recommends strategems like organizing the innovative group as a unit separate from the operating group. "Whenever we have tried to make the existing unit the carrier of the entrepreneurial project, we have failed." Even giants can innovate—but only by deliberately practicing "entrepreneurial management," which he refuses to see as an oxymoron.

*Innovation and Entrepreneurship* is not meant to be an historical analysis. Still, it is odd that Drucker leaves out the role government played in the entrepreneurial high-tech revolution during these years; one would have thought the ideological irony of the thing would have drawn him irresistibly. As Manuel Castells argues in Volume 1 of his authoritative account of the information age, *The Rise of the Network Society,* the real entrepreneur was the taxpayer:

> [D]uring the decisive 1950s and 1960s, military contracts and the space program were essential markets for the electronics industry, both for the giant defense contractors of Southern California and for the start-up innovators of Silicon Valley and New England. They could not have survived without the generous funding and protected markets of a U.S. government anxious to recover technological superiority over the Soviet Union. . . . Genetic engineering, spun off from major research universities, hospitals, and health research institutes, was largely funded and sponsored by government money. Thus the state, not the innovative entrepreneur in his garage, both in America and throughout the world, was the initiator of the Information Technology Revolution.[18]

Finally, from the perspective of the 1980s, what's striking about *Innovation and Entrepreneurship* is its sunny attitude toward the new jobs created by entrepreneurs from the 1960s to the 1980s. These are the same jobs, after all, that gave rise during the 1992 and 1996 presidential campaigns to one-liners like, "Yah, I've heard the politicians talking about all those new jobs out there, and they're right; there are a lot of jobs—I've got *three* of them." Junk jobs they are called, and you need three of them to get the wages once provided by one job. "60 percent of the jobs created in the past year," the *Wall Street Journal* reported of 1993, "are in three industries; health care, restaurants and bars, and temporary help. Some of these are good jobs. But the average restaurant job pays only $5.53 an hour. Temporary jobs offer little security and often no health benefits." From 1994 through April 1997, the *New York Times* reports, the economy generated 19,000 jobs "in well-paid fields like manufacturing . . . while it created 428,000 retail store jobs. . . ."

Yes, the entrepreneur flourished. Many of his employees were (and are) not so lucky, however. "Both large firms and unions are playing a reduced role in employment," the economist Robert Z. Lawrence notes. "As a result, fewer workers are having their pay determined by prevailing bargains and norms, while more are subject to the vagaries and idiosyncrasies of practices in smaller firms," partly because small businesses typically pay lower wages than big companies. In the years of the jobs boom the U.S. went from having an economy in which the union wage put upward pressure on all wages to an economy in which too few workers receive the union wage for it to have that tonic effect. Not coincidentally, in the same years the U.S. went from broad democratic prosperity toward an *Apartheid Economy*, to use the title of a recent article in the *Harvard Business Review* from which I have removed the question mark after "Economy." The author, Richard B. Freeman, a Harvard economist, describes an economy of rising inequality and stagnant real wages in which the few prosper, while the many (inflation-adjusted incomes fell for the bottom 60 percent of families in the period 1989–1997) fall further and further behind. So, yes, two cheers for the entrepreneur, but first a Druckerian question: What social value can his success really have in an Apartheid Economy?[19]

*   *   *

AT A time when voting sometimes and "paying taxes all the time" defines the experience of public life for most Americans, how can we fashion a richer civic identity? Consumers, employees, parents, how many of us, in more than a famished sense, are citizens? How can we gain a voice in politics and government, at work, in our local communities? Where can we find the moral forge of solidarity?

Early in his career Drucker thought he had the answer to questions like these: through our role as employees in the enterprise or organization we can be industrial citizens in the industrial society. But as the relative stability of the age of Keynes gave way to the creative destruction of the age of Schumpeter, Drucker had to abandon that idea; the enterprise was a vessel of change not of continuity. From *The End of Economic Man* forward, Drucker has insisted on the need for a strong noneconomic society to make "inequality appear far less intolerable" and to shore people up against the nihilism of the market. Inequality grows; nihilism thrives. A social space where money does not rule—we have never needed it more.[20]

Drucker has not just theorized about that space; for fifty years he has worked to create and expand it. Though his long *pro bono* association with nonprofit organizations and community groups he has sought to change the world not just to understand it.

To carry his counsel beyond his clients, in the early 1990s Drucker published *Managing the Non-Profit Organization*. In his long 1994 *Atlantic* essay, "The Age of Social Transformation," he also gave his fullest account of the role of noneconomic satisfactions in today's knowledge society.

"[T]he essence of the knowledge society," he writes, "is mobility in terms of where one lives, mobility in terms of what one does, mobility in terms of one's affiliation." This mobility comes at the cost of "roots," "neighborhood," and the organic solidarity of "community." Mobility—also brings new social challenges and tasks.

The knowledge society will inevitably become far more competitive than any society we have yet known—for the simple reason that with knowledge being universally accessible, there are no excuses for nonperformance. . . . It is a society in which many more people than ever before can be successful. But it is therefore, by definition, also a society in which many more people can fail, or at least come in second.[21]

With traditional community shattered by mobility, "Who then, in the knowledge society, takes care of the social tasks"—poverty, family disintegration, drug addiction, homelessness, crime; and how can the failure endemic to the knowledge society be solaced?

The twentieth century has given two still-applicable answers, "a majority answer and a dissenting opinion. Both have been proven to be the wrong answers."[22]

Drucker gave the dissenting opinion in the *Future of Industrial Man:* The large corporate enterprise would recreate community, would become "the place in which and through which the social tasks would be organized." In the disappointment of Drucker's career, this "has not worked." "It's time to give up thinking of jobs or career paths as we once did and think in terms of taking on assignments one after the other," he told T. George Harris, former editor of the *Harvard Business Review* in 1993. "The stepladder is gone, and there is not even the implied structure of an industry's rope ladder. It's more like vines and you bring your own machete."

Drucker thinks the downsizing wave of the early and mid 1990s— IBM's cutting of 85,000 employees, General Motors of 74,000, Sears of 50,000—has all but destroyed the ethic of loyalty among middle managers. Tom Peters sums up the postdownsizing idea of loyalty this way: "We are CEO's of our own companies: Me Inc. To be in business today, our most important job is to be head marketer for the brand called You." "People need to look at themselves as self-employed, as vendors who came to this company to sell their skills," says James Meadows, a vice president of AT&T, laying out the assumption behind his company's 1996 decision to lay off 13 percent of its workforce. In *Corporate Executions,* Alan Downs, a management consultant with the candor of Machiavelli, expresses the cold logic of downsizing: "Employees are interchangeable components that can be plugged in wherever and whenever they are needed. When the immediate demand for their services has subsided, they can be discarded." Nothing could be further removed from Drucker's teaching to regard the employee not as a cost to cut but as a resource to preserve.

As for the economic results of downsizing, the American Management Association, according to *The Economist,* reports that "fewer than half of the firms that have downsized since 1990 have seen long-term improvements in quality, profitability or productivity."

Looming large behind what the historian Nicholas Mills calls "Corporate Darwinism" are impatient shareholders, pension funds included. For the sake of retired workers, the jobs of currently employed workers are put at risk. But the real beneficiaries of shareholder capitalism are still those who own the bulk of the shares. From 1989 to 1995, stock ownership increased from 31 to 41 percent of all families, according to a recent Federal Reserve report. But only 29 percent of all families own more than $2,000 worth of stock, whether through 401 (k) pensions or direct purchase, while the top 5 percent of families own half of all stock. They, not middle-class workers through their pension funds, are shareholder capitalism's big gainers. "In the 1990s," Mills writes in *The Triumph of Meanness,* "the ultimate significance of a corporate culture that makes allegiance to the shareholder so dominant is that anything goes." Drucker captures the new reality in a characteristically sharp metaphor: "Corporations once built to last like pyramids are now more like tents."

The second answer is that government will perform the social tasks left by the waning of community and the weakening of the family and neighborhood support systems. This has been "totally disproven" (the "totally" of conversation). Government should set policy and provide funding. "But as the agency to *run* social services, it has proven itself almost totally incompetent. . . ."

In fact the social tasks will be met neither by the private nor the public sector but by "a separate and new *social sector.*" There are about one million nonprofit or charitable organizations doing "social sector work" in the U.S. Nearly 70 percent, Drucker says, started since the 1960s. Those years also saw the rise of the knowledge society, when social problems worsened and knowledge work left millions needing noneconomic associations and satisfactions. Feeding the hungry, housing the homeless, healing the sick, teaching the young, strengthening communities and families, the social sector has done the country signal service. "Government . . . makes rules and enforces them. Business expects to be paid: it supplies. The social sector institutions aim at *changing the human being.*"[23]

That is their main purpose; more and more, "they serve a second and equally important purpose. *They create citizenship.* . . . As a volunteer in the social sector institution, the individual can again make a difference." And, through churches and other nonprofit organizations, nearly 100 million Americans volunteer an average of three hours each week—making the nonprofit sector "America's largest employer." In the next century nonprofit institutions will contract with government to accomplish social tasks. And they will also give millions of their volunteer knowledge workers "a sphere in which . . . they can create community."[24]

In Drucker's tomorrow, knowledge workers will find meaning and community through volunteer work in social sector organizations, while those served by the organizations will benefit from a delivery system at once caring *and* efficient. But *who* will those people be? In the media coverage of the "volunteer summit" held in 1997 in Philadelphia one heard it said repeatedly that only a very few social sector organizations and volunteers work on the problems of the inner city.

These problems, Drucker notes in his *Atlantic* essay, should be seen in the context of changes in the labor market, which in turn flow from changes in the unreachably removed world economy—which indicates the scope of difficulty in making progress on them. A generation ago young African-American men could get good-paying mass-production jobs. But, Drucker writes, "the fall of the industrial worker hits America's Blacks disproportionately hard—quantitatively, but qualitatively even more. It denigrates what has been the most potent role model in the Black community in America: the well-paid industrial worker with high job security, full health insurance, and a guaranteed retirement pension—yet possessing neither skill nor much education." In his 1996 book, *When Work Disappears,* the Harvard sociologist William J. Wilson, offers much the same analysis: The economic freedom that has bid up the wages of the top 25 percent of Americans has come at the price of blue-collar industrial jobs in the cities. Wilson sees a WPA-style jobs program as the only solution scaled to the problems of the inner city. Clearly, anything of that scope is beyond the social sector. And there is a danger, in the celebration of the social sector and its volunteerism, that the taxpayer will get the highly agreeable message that the problems of the inner city can be met without his taxes. That is an expedient delusion. In her 1997 book, *It Takes a Nation,* Rebecca Blank, a Northwestern University economist, calculates that to replace the $77 billion spent annually by the federal government on welfare, food stamps, and cash assistance to the elderly poor through the religious community

... requires that every one of the 258,000 religious congregations (Catholic, Protestant, Jewish, Muslim or otherwise) that exist in this country would have to raise an additional $300,000 per year in all future years . . . and spend all of the increase on services for the poor. Alternatively, if this is done through private charitable organizations that serve the poor, it would require those groups to raise over *seven* times more in private donations than they currently receive.[25]

JUST AS he saw management behind the entrepreneurial boom, so Drucker credits management for the growth and success of nonprofits. "Fifty years ago," he writes, "'management' was a very bad word in nonprofit organizations. It meant 'business' to them, and the one thing they were not was a business. . . . After all, they did not have a 'bottom line.'" But that attitude belongs to the past. An increase in donations does not account for nonprofit successes; Americans give about the same percentage of their income as they have done for years, he points out in *The New Realities* (1989). "They are based on greatly increased productivity. Third sector institutions—or at least a large number of them—get more results out of the same resources. The growth of the third sector is primarily a management achievement." Note the succinct definition of management's function there, to get more results out of the same resources.[26]

Partly to dispel any lingering nonprofit dubiety about management, Drucker wrote *Managing the Non-Profit Organization* (1990), doing for the nonprofits what he had done for management and entrepreneurship. An accurate review in the *New York Times* called it "an engaging book" that "offers managers in the nonprofit sector the kind of vigorous, sensible, mind-stretching advice that has won him a reputation as the most stimulating management thinker of his time."[27]

Reading *Managing the Non-Profit Organization* is like attending a reunion of old classmates: here is "who is the customer?," here is the stress on "results," over here is the counsel to "start out with what the person has done well," and here are two old friends, leadership "by example" and "look always at performance, not at promise." No sententious sage, Drucker dispenses practical advice that real people can use—the book distills fifty years of experience with nonprofits. Don't moralize mere effort, he instructs these high-minded organizations. Try a strategy or an action once, twice—then try something else. "There is only so much time and so many resources. . . . You can see some great achievements where people labored in the wilderness for twenty-five years. But they are very rare. Most of the people who persist in the wilderness leave nothing behind but bleached bones." On fund raising he complains that the nonprofits "still believe that the way to get money is to hawk *needs*. But the American public gives to *results*. It no longer gives to charity; it 'buys in'." And don't regard people who give as "donors"; they are "contributors," to be treated as long-term members of your organization. Ideally, contributors should "see support of the institution as self-fulfillment"—a challenge to marketing. It's sound public policy, he argues, to allow taxpayers to deduct $1.10 for each dollar they give to a nonprofit organization, "for a well-managed nonprofit [organization] gets at least twice the bang out of each buck than a government agency does." The father of "privatization" urges the unfortunate "nonprofitization" to replace "mismanagement by welfare bureaucracies."[28]

Intended for use, *Managing the Non-Profit Organization* is not without entertainment value. Drucker tells an anecdote about the German ambassador to London around the turn of the century who "resigned his ambassadorship because the new English king, Edward VII, was a notorious womanizer who liked the diplomatic corps to give him stag parties at which the most popular London courtesans would pop naked out of cakes. The ambassador said he was not willing to see a pimp when he saw himself in the mirror shaving in the morning." His deci-

sion to resign was "the essence of leadership," Drucker says, and a para-
ble for leaders and executives. "You are visible; you'd better realize that
you are constantly on trial. The rule is: I don't want to see a pimp in
the mirror when I shave in the morning." Leaders lead by the infec-
tious example of integrity, not by charisma.[29]

Post-Capitalist Society, published in 1993, is the most revealing title on the Drucker shelf. "[A]lthough I believe in the free market," he says, "I have serious reservations about capitalism." Indeed, for
sixty years Drucker has sought to take the capital out of capitalism.
Roll his career backward and it leaps out at you like a tiger from a tree.
Whether with the nonprofit, the plant community, the manager, the
responsible worker, executive compensation, or status, function, and
legitimacy, Drucker discusses economic life in terms of values, integrity, character, knowledge, vision, responsibility, self-control, social
integration, teamwork, community, competence, social responsibility,
the quality of life, self-fulfillment, leadership, duty, purpose, dignity,
meaning—but rarely money. He defends profit, but as if it were broc-
coli: a distasteful obligation of managers who would rather be reading
Kierkegaard. He praises executives like Max De Pree who tie their pay
to comparatively modest multiples of employee pay, while he depicts
the kings of inequality, the much larger corps of executives with their
pay 200 or 300 times their average worker's, as corrupt. He prizes economic freedom but its full consequences lie heavily on his heart, and
he is ever on the hunt for noneconomic motives and satisfactions. The
biggest capitalists on Wall Street, he exults, are no longer tycoons in tall
hats: "Pension-fund capitalism is capitalism sans the capitalists." The
purpose of a business, finally, is nothing so crass as to make a profit
(though there's nothing wrong with that, mind you), but to "create a
customer." This "business philosopher," "management guru," this
"man who invented the corporate society" is morally uneasy with the

fire of American striving, the manifest content of the American Dream.

In *Post-Capitalist Society,* he sees capitalism off altogether, announcing that capital's central place in the economy is being taken by . . . Knowledge! "That knowledge has become *the* resource, rather than *a* resource, is what makes our society 'post-capitalist'."[30]

How did knowledge come to play this central economic role? Up until the early modern period knowledge applied to *being.* "Then almost overnight, it came to be applied to *doing,*" Drucker writes. "It became a resource and a utility." The Industrial Revolution applied knowledge to tools; Frederick W. Taylor's productivity revolution applied knowledge to work; and the managerial revolution of the mid-twentieth century applied knowledge to knowledge. ("The right definition of a manager is one who 'is responsible for the application and performance of knowledge.'") The postwar GI Bill democratized knowledge. "The G.I. Bill of Rights—and the enthusiastic response to it on the part of America's veterans—signaled the shift to the knowledge society. Future historians may consider it the most important event of the twentieth century. We are clearly in the middle of this transformation; indeed, if history is any guide, it will not be completed until 2010 or 2020. But already it has changed the political, economic, and moral landscape of the world." The knowledge worker today, the knowledge society in 2020.[31]

The knowledge society will face two serious problems, one economic, one social.

This society in which knowledge workers dominate is in danger of a new "class conflict" between the large minority of knowledge workers and the majority of people who will make their living through traditional ways, either by manual work . . . or by service work. The productivity of knowledge work—still abysmally low—will predictably become the *eco-*

> ### The Educated Person
>
> "If the feudal knight was the clearest embodiment of society in the early Middle Ages, and the 'bourgeois' under Capitalism, the educated person will represent society in the post-capitalist society in which knowledge has become the central resource."
>
> —*Post-Capitalist Society* (1993)

*nomic* challenge of the knowledge society. . . . The productivity of the non-knowledge service worker will increasingly become the *social* challenge of the knowledge society. On it will depend the ability of the knowledge society to give decent incomes, and with them dignity and status, to nonknowledge people.[32]

That is the peril of the knowledge society; its promise is that it will be the "first society in which ordinary common people—and that means most people—do not earn their daily bread by the sweat of their brow. It is the first society in which 'honest work' does not mean a callused hand." This is far more than a social change. "It is a change in the *human condition.*"

AFTER THE publication of *Post-Capitalist Society* Drucker sat for an interview with *Industry Week.* The interviewer asked him if he thought his books had been understood—what effects did he think they had had? Much as a poet might speak of his influence on other poets, Drucker spoke first of his influence on other continents.

*Q:* What about the United States?

*A:* My impression is that managers in the United States have derived two major points from my writing and counsel. First, they at least started to understand that people are a resource and not just a cost. . . . Which raises the second major point that managers here seem to note about my work, that I helped them start to *see* management. . . . I think that many credit me with discovering the discipline and insisting that businesses take management seriously—as a profession that can make a difference in the life of the business.

I would hope that American managers—indeed, managers world-wide—continue to appreciate what I have been saying almost from day one: that management is so much more than exercising rank and privi-lege, that it is so much more than "making deals." Management affects people and their lives.[33]

# 9

# "God Does Not Need a Management Consultant"

"We didn't bring our bathing suits," one of the three visitors from New York replied. They had spent a hot morning thinking through the challenges of their new business with the Sage of Claremont, who had just invited them for a swim in his backyard pool. "I don't have one, either," Drucker said. "But we are all men."

They were enjoying themselves in the pool when Doris Drucker arrived home. "Doris?" Peter called into the house for her. "Please come out and meet these interesting young men."

Consulting with Peter Drucker is an experience to remember. Anyone meeting him for the first time is likely to be intimidated by his books, his fame, his client list—he could be spending his time with a *Fortune* 500 CEO instead of spending it with you. But the benignity of Drucker's furrowed smile quickly makes you feel at ease. Tall, though slightly bent with age, and slender, with a sun-browned face and nobly bald pate, Drucker makes his strongest impression through a deep accented voice he uses to dramatic effect. His "No," for example, as in, "Nooo . . . You . . . are . . . wrong," is said with a comic inflection and timing that unstings the judgment. He has, you sense, reserves of Old World charm sufficient to smooth any troubled waters. All of Europe went into the making of Peter Drucker: droll, urbane, with an intelli-

gence irradiated by sophistication, his persona captures the sparkle and
dash of a piece by Johann Strauss, a fellow subject of that tragic con-
fection, the Austro-Hungarian Empire.

According to several of his clients, Drucker characteristically takes
the issue or problem that brought you to him, loses it in festoons of
talk that seem to touch on everything *but* your problem, and then, near
the end of the day, returns it to you, unsolved but altered by the company it's kept in his mind. "Putting it in perspective" is the phrase his
clients use. "You end up looking at problems and opportunities in a
different way," one says. "He thinks outside the dots." Another echoes
that sentiment: "He makes you see the whys to the issue and not just
the answer." Drucker views his consulting sessions as a form of teaching. What he teaches may apply to your organization or it may apply to
you as an executive or even to your qualities as a human being. And
"it" is an insight, a way of seeing, not a fact-heavy analysis. One client
spent three years trying to grasp that when Drucker said, "You know,
Don, people have no imagination," he meant, Don't assume your service is so obviously wonderful to others as it is to you. Don had to *market* it.

Of course most of Drucker's advice does not take three years to
understand—make that *really* understand. The American Heart Association, according to Dudley Hafner, its former president, altered its entire field operation after Drucker outlined for Hafner the organization
plan the British used to govern India with only a thousand young men.
"We redefined ourselves as an information organization," Hafner says.
He calls Drucker "an inspired painter of concepts." At their first meeting he was as surprised to learn that Drucker had gone door-to-door in
his neighborhood collecting money for the American Heart Association as we are.

Drucker says he charges enough—a reported $6,000 to $8,000 a
day—so his corporate clients will take what he says seriously. "It was

worth a great deal to have Peter Drucker be enthusiastic about our start-up," one satisfied customer testifies. On the same principle Drucker asks his *pro bono* clients to write him checks for the full amount of his fee, then mails the checks right back.

Asked to name the best piece of advice Drucker has given him, Bill Pollard, CEO of a worldwide building maintenance business, tells of a serendipitous meeting with Drucker in the lobby of a Tokyo hotel. Drucker was in Tokyo lecturing for his Japanese clients, Pollard to straighten out some serious trouble with his Japanese partner. Piqued, he was close to scrapping the relationship. "I'm not even going to go down and visit him in Osaka," he told Drucker. "Worst thing you could do, Bill," Drucker, speaking "in his deep Viennese brogue," adjured him. "You get on that train the first thing tomorrow morning and go down there and eat a little crow." Drucker was calling on his decades-long experience of Japan. Pollard, knowing this, did as Drucker directed. He made that train. By losing face himself, he spared his partner humiliation. Their relationship rapidly improved.

Drucker possesses a famous collection of Japanese art, and taught the subject on the side at Claremont College for five years. He not only collects Japanese art; he has sought to help American institutions and museums dedicated to Japanese art, giving donations to teaching programs at Harvard's Fogg Museum and the University of Michigan and volunteering his counsel to Japan House in New York and the Asian Art Museum in San Francisco. Rand Castile, the former director of both institutions, says that Drucker saved the latter. By the mid-1970s, the San Francisco museum was moribund. Concerned about the deterioration of a cross-cultural institution in an emerging global civilization, Drucker took it upon himself to come to its rescue. "Peter inspired us with his vision of what a museum like ours should be and we began to convey that to donors," Castile says. Drucker allowed the mayor of San Francisco to appoint him to the museum's Board of Directors. His name on the museum's letterhead, his willingness to give lectures, gratis, to potential corporate contributors, and his strategic advice on fund raising were decisive. Over nine years the museum increased its endowment from $3 million to $40 million, including a "very large" donation from Peter Drucker himself.

Drucker mounted a similar one-man rescue of CARE at a time when it was reeling from a financial scandal. "There is a direct link between Peter Drucker and children in need throughout the world," says Bill Johnston, former president of CARE. Drucker called his autobiography *Adventures of a Bystander,* but these are hardly the actions of a bystander.

At the culture's other pole, Drucker has also counseled major league baseball teams. When he was managing the New York Mets, Yogi Berra, then Drucker's neighbor in Montclair, New Jersey, came to Drucker with a delicate off-field problem. "Peter," Drucker recalls him saying, "I can handle the baseball, but what can I do about the whores?" Young, rich, totally inexperienced, the players drew groupies who kept them out late and parted them from quantities of their money. Drucker advised Berra to hire a former nun or a retired Army sergeant to shoo away the groupies. Berra did and it worked.

Drucker jokes that he is more an "insultant" than a consultant and that he "scolds clients for a fee." But the clients say otherwise. Uniformly, they speak of how much Drucker matters not only to their businesses but to their lives. "He makes you feel better about yourself," says Don Mitchell, a small businessman who consults with Drucker three times a year. He has that rare gift of the heart.

"I GUESS it was about six years ago that I saw an article Drucker had written about market research," Vincent Barabba says, "and I work with market research and Drucker had got a key point wrong." Barabba, the General Manager of General Motors' Knowledge Network, wrote Drucker a letter setting him right. Having long since ripened into a wisdom that welcomes correction, Drucker wrote back warmly, expressing an interest in renewing his old acquaintance with GM.

Barabba got out a 1972 edition of *Concept of the Corporation* to which Drucker had written an introduction relating how GM had spurned the book. "Frankly, I was embarrassed," Barabba says. "I took it to our chairman," who was preparing to lecture on GM's history. He liked the idea of asking Drucker to Detroit as a gesture of acknowledgment. Thus it was that a GM company plane picked up the Druckers in California, dropped Doris in Denver to hike in the Rockies, and flew on to Detroit with Peter.

He spent three days there, meeting with senior management and the GM Board of Directors, discussing the challenges of the car business today. When someone sounded a defensive note about GM's record on innovation, Drucker gently reproved him. "General Motors innovated American business!" he said, going down the list of GM's innovations in organization, strategy, accounting and other areas. It must have made the GM people proud to hear Drucker descant upon GM's historic contributions, telling of Donaldson Brown and Charles Wilson and "Mr." Sloan.

Of course Drucker also had ideas about the future of GM, so Barabba asked him to respond to an important in-house strategic paper. "We learned a lot from him," Barabba says. "His depth of understanding just blows you away." Regularly, GM bounces ideas off Drucker. After a long hiatus, he has returned to the company to which he owes his career.

PETER DRUCKER calls the emergence of the large pastoral church—the "megachurch" in mediaese—"the most significant social event in America today." He is its intellectual godfather; he's been tu-

toring it for years through the agency of Bob Buford, a highly successful Dallas-based television executive who in 1985 founded the Leadership Network. "His Leadership Network," Drucker writes in his
preface to Buford's 1994 book *Half Time: Changing Your Game Plan from
Success to Significance,* "worked as a catalyst to make the large, pastoral
churches work effectively, to identify their main problems, to make
them capable of perpetuating themselves (as no earlier pastoral church
has ever been able to do), and to focus them on their mission as apos-
tles, witnesses, and central community services." Modest, Buford says,
"I'm the legs for his brain."

Drucker, Vincent Barabba points out, appreciates the uses of big-
ness. "There are some things an elephant can do that a mouse cannot
do," he says. Through its very scale—as many as 10,000 members per
institution—the megachurch can provide social services of all kinds.
Recreating the American community eroded by the acids of modernity, the large pastoral church is realizing Peter Drucker's dream of a
new postmodern social form based on commitment instead of conformity.

IN 1981 Frances Hesselbein, the National Executive Director
of the Girl Scouts, went to a dinner in New York at which Drucker
was to be the featured speaker. She was early, alone in the big room
with the bartender. Then, aware of someone standing behind her, she
turned around. "I am Peee-tah Drooker," he said, extending his hand.

It was the beginning of a fruitful relationship, Drucker giving one
or two days a year to the Girl Scouts. "He helped us define our mission," Hesselbein says, "and especially to increase our minority enrollment."

In 1990 Hesselbein and Buford, with other Drucker alumni decided to institutionalize something of Drucker's counsel so that other
nonprofit organizations could plumb that unique resource as they had.

The Drucker Foundation would be an anomaly—a foundation that did not donate money but rather served as a knowledge bank for nonprofit organizations. Hesselbein and Buford approached Drucker with their plan to perpetuate his work and memory. That could be a delicate subject with someone of his years but Drucker, who says he is well aware that "God does not need a management consultant," is no ordinary man. "You'll be the president," he told Hesselbein, who had just retired from the Girl Scouts, "or it won't work." She has been president ever since.

Through two annual conferences, through books and tapes and a quarterly journal, *From Leader to Leader,* The Drucker Foundation "presents the best thinking and practices, and their applications to the social sector." Drucker has dedicated the royalties from *Managing the Non-Profit Organization,* $250,000 so far, to The Drucker Foundation, which gives a yearly $25,000 Drucker Award for Nonprofit Innovation—293 programs applied in 1996. The one chosen was Second Family; a program of the Lutheran Church of Illinois, it helps HIV-infected parents make plans to place their children with other families before they die. If placement with an extended family is not possible, Second Family allows the birth parent to choose from a pool of prospective parents whom it has trained "to care for special mental and physical needs that children in this situation may have." Something of Peter Drucker will always be with these children.

ON NEW Year's Day 1950, Peter drove his father Adolph Drucker to visit Joseph Schumpeter, then in his last year of teaching at Harvard and in rapidly failing health (he died eight days later). He and Adolph reminisced about their young days in Vienna in the vanished world of "prewar," the incessant talk of which had driven young Peter Drucker out on his long journey toward a wholly significant life. The conversation took a more serious turn when Schumpeter, answering a question from Adolph, said: "You know, Adolph, I have now reached the age where I know that it is not enough to be remembered for books and theories. One does not make a difference unless it is a difference in people's lives." Drucker says he has "never forgotten that conversation." It gave him the measure of his achievement.

# Notes

## Chapter 1: A Singular Education

1. Peter F. Drucker, *The Frontiers of Management* (New York: Harper & Row, 1986), pp. 15–16. Also, interview with Drucker, April 1995; letter from Drucker, March 19, 1997.

2. Peter F. Drucker, *Adventures of a Bystander* (New Brunswick, NJ: Transaction Publishers, 1994), p. 35.

3. Ibid., p. 35.

4. James O'Toole, review of *The Leader of the Future,* edited by Peter F. Drucker for the 1996 ASAP Conference Board, *Across the Board,* May 1996.

5. Ibid., p. 5. Also Peter F. Drucker, *Landmarks of Tomorrow* (New Brunswick, NJ: Transaction Publishers, 1996), p. 269.

6. "Hoover" is from a personal letter from Peter F. Drucker to the author dated August 27, 1996; *Adventures,* p. 3; Interview with Drucker, December 1995; Peter F. Drucker, *Managing in a Time of Great Change* (New York: Dutton, 1995), pp. 344–45; for "grandmother," see "The Memoirs of a Renaissance Man," in *Business Week,* March 19, 1997, p. 10.

7. Drucker, *Bystander,* pp. 89, 91.

8. Drucker, *Landmarks,* p. 203; Drucker, *Great Change,* p. 220; Drucker, *Adventures,* pp. 53–54, and p. 101; for Gustav see John J. Tarrant, *Drucker: The Man Who Invented Corporate Society* (Boston: Cahners Books, 1976), p. 101.

9. Peter F. Drucker, *Drucker on Asia* (London: Butterworth-Heinemann, 1997), p. 105; Robert Lenzner and Stephan S. Johnson, "Seeing Things As They Really Are," *Forbes,* March 1997; Peter F. Drucker, *The Practice of Management* (New York: HarperCollins, 1993), p. 46; "Peter Drucker, Salvationist," *The Economist,* Fall 1997, p. 83; Peter F. Drucker, *The New Realities* (New York: HarperCollins, 1989), p. 136.

10. Drucker, *Adventures,* p. 68.

11. Ibid., pp. 65, 62, 66.

12. Drucker, *Adventures,* pp. 72, 24, 75; "The Invention of Management," *Directors and Boards,* Winter 1982, pp. 14–21 (Warren Bennis interviews Peter Drucker).

13. Peter F. Drucker, *The Age of Discontinuity* (New Brunswick, NJ: Transaction Publishers, 1994), p. 360. Peter F. Drucker, *The New Society* (New Brunswick, NJ: Transaction Publishers, 1993), p. 189; for credentialism, see Drucker, *The New Realities,* p. 244.; for "meritocracy," see Drucker, *Great Change,* p. 8.

14. Drucker, *Adventures,* p. 70; Drucker, *Landmarks,* p. 148; Drucker letter to author of August 28, 1996.

15. Peter F. Drucker, *Managing the Non-Profit Organization* (New York: HarperCollins, 1990), pp. 201, 202.

16. Drucker, *Adventures,* p. 15; Elizabeth Barker, *Austria: 1918–1972* (Miami: University of Miami Press, 1973), p. 4; A. J. P. Taylor, *From Napoleon to the Second International* (New York: Penguin, 1994), pp. 388–89; p. 127; *Adventures,* pp. 105–107.

17. Drucker, *Drucker on Asia,* p. 102; Drucker, *Innovation and Entrepreneurship* (New York: HarperCollins, 1993), p. 46; Drucker in letter to author, August 28, 1996; Drucker, *Adventures,* p. 107.

18. Drucker, *Drucker on Asia,* pp. 102, 104, 105.

19. Drucker, *Adventures,* p. 123; Peter F. Drucker, *The Ecological Vision* (New Brunswick, NJ: Transaction Publishers, 1993), p. 451.

20. Drucker in letter to author, August 28, 1996; Interview with Peter F. Drucker, in Claremont, CA, November 1996; Drucker, *Drucker on Asia,* p. 106.

21. Interview with Peter F. Drucker, in Claremont, CA, December 1995; Drucker, *Drucker on Asia,* p. 106; *Forbes,* March 1997; Peter F. Drucker, *Managing the Non-Profit,* p. 224; Peter F. Drucker, "My Life as a Knowledge Worker" (*B. H. Business Book,* Feb. 1997), pp. 76–82.

22. Drucker, *Landmarks,* pp. 141–42; Drucker, *Frontiers,* p. 227.

23. Drucker in letter to author, August 28, 1996; Berthold Freyberg, "The Genesis of Drucker's Thought," in *Peter Drucker: Contributions to Business Enterprise,* edited by Tony H. Bonaparte and John E. Flaherty (New York: New York University Press, 1970), p. 18.

24. Drucker, *The Ecological Vision,* p. 442.

25. Drucker, *Adventures,* pp. 160–61.

26. Peter F. Drucker, *The End of Economic Man* (New Brunswick, NJ: Transaction Publishers, 1995), pp. 13, 14, 23.

27. Drucker, *Adventures,* p. 162.

28. Doris Drucker, "Invent Radium or I'll Pull Your Hair," a memoir to be published in the *Atlantic Monthly* in 1998.

29. Drucker, *Adventures,* p. 25.

30. Drucker in letter to author, August 28, 1996; Drucker, *Adventures,* 187.

31. Drucker, *The Ecological Vision,* pp. 75–76; Drucker, *Frontiers,* p. 14; "An Interview With Drucker," in Bonaparte Flaherty, op. cit., p. 324.

32. "Solve the future," from Peter F. Drucker, *The Future of Industrial Man* (New Brunswick, NJ: Transaction Publishers, 1995), p. 181; B. Alterlund, "Peter F. Drucker," *Wilson Library Bulletin,* January 1943, p. 368; Drucker in letter to author, August 28, 1996.

## Chapter 2: "I Write"

1. Drucker, *The Ecological Vision,* p. 441; "five or six," phone interview with Drucker, December 1997.

2. The account of Drucker's production is taken from an April 14, 1997 letter from Drucker to the author; "I write" from *The Ecological Vision,* p. 441.

3. Drucker's leisure from Drucker, *Frontiers,* p. 12.

4. Peter F. Drucker, *The Effective Executive* (New York: Harper & Row, 1985), p. 25; Tarrant, p. 131.

5. Drucker, *The Ecological Vision,* p. 456.

6. For surgeons and barbers, see Drucker, *Practice,* p. 193; for Watson, see "IBM's Watson: Vision for Tomorrow" in Drucker, *Frontiers,* p. 275.

7. Epithets from Drucker, *The Age of Discontinuity,* p. 192; Drucker, *The New Realities,* p. 245; Drucker, *Landmarks,* p. 93 and p. 156; Drucker, *Adventures,* p. 249; Drucker, *The Ecological Vision,* p. 62; Peter F. Drucker, *Management: Tasks, Responsibilities, Practices* (New York: HarperCollins, 1993), p. 717; Drucker, *Practice,* p. 389.

8. Alan M. Kantrow, "Why Read Peter Drucker?" in *Harvard Business Review,* January–February, 1980, p. 75; for "peasants," see "Drucker's Supreme Folly," *Los Angeles Times,* in Letters to the Editor, Business, November 8, 1987; for "see," see Drucker, *The New Realities,* p. 264.

9. Drucker, *Great Change,* p. 259.

10. Drucker, *The End of Economic Man,* p. 218.

11. Peter F. Drucker, *Managing for the Future* (New York: Dutton, 1992), p. 208.

12. "single one," from *Economic Man,* p. 227; "every," from Drucker, *Economic Man,* p. 142; "no one," from Drucker, *The New Society,* p. xii.

13. Drucker, *Managing for the Future,* p. 281; ibid., p. 265; Drucker, *Great Change,* p. 45; "Three Popular Explanations," from Drucker, *Management: Tasks, Responsibilities, Practices,* p. 137; ibid., p. 694; Drucker, *Great Change,* p. 257; Drucker, *Management,* p. 568.

14. Drucker, *Industrial Man,* p. 88; Drucker, *Great Change,* p. 89; Drucker, *The New Realities,* p. 100; Drucker, *Industrial Man,* p. 90.

15. Drucker, *Management,* pp. 280, 327, 369, 416, 476, 479.

16. Drucker, *The Age of Discontinuity,* p. 83.

17. Tarrant, p. 157.

18. Drucker, *Post-Capitalist Society* (New York: Harper & Row, 1993), p. 184.

19. Tarrant, p. 197. Drucker, *The New Realities,* p. 61; Drucker, *The Ecological Vision,* p. 449; ibid., p. 317; ibid., p. 361; ibid., p. 361; Drucker, *Landmarks,* p. ix; Drucker, *The Ecological Vision,* p. 447; Drucker, *Landmarks,* p. 4; Drucker, *The Age of Discontinuity,* p. x.

20. Kantrow, pp. 76–77, 79; for "never learned anything out of a book," see Warren Bennis interview with Drucker, "The Invention of Management," in *Directors & Boards,* Winter 1982, p. 15.

21. Drucker, *Frontiers,* p. x.

## Chapter 3: In Search of the New Society

1. Drucker, *Adventures,* pp. 256, 308. For "failure" see for example, Drucker's Epilogue to *Concept of the Corporation* (New Brunswick, NJ: Transaction Publishers, 1993), p. 305, which also covers Japan point.

2. Drucker, *The End of Economic Man,* pp. ix, xxxvi.

3. Ibid., pp. 7, 24, 25.

4. Drucker, *Industrial Man,* p. 47; Drucker, *Economic Man,* pp. 40, 50.

5. Drucker, *Industrial Man,* pp. 25, 35; Drucker, *Adventures,* p. 113.

6. "Germanicus," *Germany—The Last Four Years* (Boston: Houghton Mifflin, 1937), pp. 6, 27.

7. "Mugwump" is taken from a letter from Drucker to the author, April 24, 1997; for "Bagehot," see Drucker, *Ecological Vision,* p. 442; Drucker, *Landmarks,* p. 178; Peter F. Drucker, "The Age of Social Transformations," *Atlantic Monthly,* December 1994.

8. Peter F. Drucker, "Political Correctness and American Academe," in *Society,* November/December 1994, p. 60.

9. Warren Bennis interview with Drucker, in *Directors & Boards,* Winter 1982, pp. 14–21.

10. Author's interview with Drucker, December 1995.

11. Drucker, *Industrial Man,* pp. 11, 95, 90.

12. For Barzun, see jacket copy of *Industrial Man;* for Hazlitt, *The Yale Review* (Winter 1943), pp. 380–82.

13. Drucker, *Economic Man,* p. xxxvii; Drucker, *Industrial Man,* pp. 23, 13.

14. Drucker, *Economic Man,* pp. 17, 236.

15. Drucker, *Industrial Man,* pp. 10, 30, 32.

16. Ibid., p. 30.

17. For dignity and fulfillment, see Drucker, *Concept,* p. 140; for Camus, see Drucker, *Industrial Man,* p. 34. Ibid., pp. 29, 60, 85, 103, 95; for Marx see C. Wright Mills, ed., *Images of Man: The Classical Tradition in Sociological Thinking* (New York: Braziller, 1960), p. 498; Drucker, *Industrial Man,* pp. 498, 64.

18. For "justification by performance," see Drucker, *The Age of Discontinuity,* pp. 211, 204; for examples, see Drucker, *Concept,* p. 157; for can openers see Drucker, *The New Society,* p. 181.

## Chapter 4: Inside GM

1. Drucker interviewed by Warren Bennis in "The Invention of Management" in *Directors & Boards,* Winter 1982, p. 17; Drucker, *Frontiers,* p. 10.

2. Bennis interview, p. 17.

3. For Political-Theory Research, see Drucker, *Adventures,* p. 257; for Lewis Jones and Library, see Bennis interview, p. 20.

4. For Donaldson Brown, see Bennis interview, pp. 20–21; for "man," see Drucker, *Concept,* p. 61; for "violence" see Nelson Lichtenstein, *The Most Dangerous Man in Detroit* (New York: Basic Books, 1995), p. 78; for "labor spies," see Frances Fox Piven and Richard A. Cloward, *Poor People's Movements* (New York: Vintage, 1979), p. 135.

5. Drucker's profile of Alfred P. Sloan, *Fortune,* (April 23, 1990).

6. Drucker, *Adventures,* p. 279; Drucker, *The Effective Executive,* p. 135.

7. Drucker, *Adventures,* p. 287.

8. Ibid., pp. 280–81.

9. Drucker, *Concept,* pp. 46, 88, 71, 12, 222.

10. For strike, see Drucker, *Concept,* p. 199; for Reuther, see Lichtenstein, *Most Dangerous Man,* p. 105.

11. John Micklethwait and Adrian Wooldridge, *The Witch Doctors* (New York: Times Books, 1996), p. 69.

12. For 95 percent, see Drucker, *Concept,* pp. 56, 57; for lunch, see Drucker, *Adventures,* p. 266.

13. For "outsourcing," see Drucker, *Managing for the Future,* Chapter 36, "Sell the Mailroom," pp. 275–79; hospital example from author conversation with Drucker, December 1995; for "opportunities," see Drucker, *Post-Capitalist Society,* p. 95.

14. For "buggy whip," from a conversation with Drucker.

15. See Drucker, *Concept,* pp. 142, 143, 147–48, 155; for "mass production," see letter from Drucker to the author, May 14, 1997.

16. For "Coyle," see Drucker, *Adventures,* p. 294; for "Sloan," see Drucker, *Adventures,* p. 288; for Sloan conversation with Drucker, see Drucker, *Concept,* p. 307; for "Ford," see Bennis interview, p. 17.

17. Drucker, *Concept,* pp. 294, 295, 296.

18. For "apogee," see Lichetenstein, *Most Dangerous Man,* p. 234.

19. Drucker, *Concept,* p. 300.

20. Drucker, *Concept,* pp. 301–303; for "wages," see Lichtenstein, *Most Dangerous Man,* p. 176; for "Heath," see James T. Patterson, *Grand Expectations* (New York: Oxford University Press, 1996), p. 61.

21. For "Los Angeles," see General Motors article, *Wall Street Journal* (front page), March 27, 1997; for "bitter workers," see Ruth Milkman, *Farewell to the Factory: Auto Workers in the Late Twentieth Century* (Berkeley: University of California Press, 1997), pp. 27, 110; for "Wilson-Drucker," see Drucker, *Concept,* p. 319; for "$365 million," see *Wall Street Journal* article.

22. Drucker, *Concept,* p. 302.

23. Ibid., p. 194.

24. For Japan, see Drucker, *Drucker on Asia,* p. 149.

25. For "Brazilian," see William Greider, *One World: Ready or Not* (New York: Simon & Schuster, 1997), p. 64.

26. Karl Polanyi, *The Great Transformation* (Boston: Beacon Press, 1957), see Author's Acknowledgments; Drucker, *Adventures,* p. 140.

27. Drucker, *Adventures,* from the chapter on the Polanyis.

## Chapter 5: The Basic Disturbance of the Twentieth Century

1. Drucker, *Concept,* p. xiii.

2. Drucker, *The New Society,* p. xvi.

3. Daniel Bell, *The End of Ideology* (New York: The Free Press, 1962) in the essay, "Work and Its Discontents," p. 233.

4. Interview with Peter Drucker, December 1996, Claremont, CA.

5. Drucker, *The New Society,* p. xi.

6. For 1914, see Bell, *The End of Ideology,* p. 235; for "general principle," see Drucker, *The New Society,* p. 3; for Huxley, see Bell, *The End of Ideology,* p. 250.

7. Drucker, *The New Realities,* pp. 78–79; Drucker, *The New Society,* p. 22.

8. Ibid., p. 5.

9. Drucker, *Concept,* p. 266.

10. Drucker, *New Society,* p. 271.

11. Ibid., p. 16.

12. Ibid., p. 19.

13. Ibid., p. 28.

14. Ibid., pp. 31, 36.

15. Ibid., p. 41.
16. Ibid.; for "subjects," see p. 49; for "managerial attitude," see p. 158; for "incentives," see p. 49.
17. Tom Frank, "Not So Fast," in *The Boston Phoenix,* September 6, 1996, p. 23. Quoting from *New York Times* story.
18. Drucker, *New Society,* p. 164; for "wrong job," see Drucker, *Management: Tasks, Responsibilities, Practices,* p. 285; for "manipulation," see ibid., pp. 424–25.
19. Drucker, *New Society,* p. 71; "responsibility" is from Drucker, letter to author, June 1997.
20. Drucker, *New Society,* p. 76.
21. Ibid., p. 79; for "fine print," see p. 238.
22. Ibid., p. 93; Peter F. Drucker, "The Delusion of Profits" reprinted in Drucker, *The Ecological Vision,* pp. 101, 104; for "*Forbes,*" see *Forbes,* March 10, 1997, p. 124.
23. Drucker, *New Society.*
24. John J. Sweeney, *America Needs a Raise* (New York: Houghton Mifflin, 1996), p. 40; *Business Week* survey cited by Congressman David Bonior, speaking in the U.S. House of Representatives as carried by C-Span, on April 29, 1997; for Max De Pree, see Jacqueline Mitchell, "Herman Miller Links Worker-CEO Pay," in the *Wall Street Journal,* May 7, 1992, Section B, 1:4; for J. P. Morgan, see *Wired,* p. 120.
25. "A cantankerous interview with Peter Drucker," in *Wired,* August 1996, p. 120.
26. Drucker, *New Society,* p. 95; for "return to capital," see Lawrence Mishel, "Capital's Gain," in *The American Prospect* 33, July–August 1997, pp. 71, 73.
27. For "baler," see Drucker, *New Society.* pp. 180–81.
28. Drucker, *Concept,* p. 207.
29. Robert L. Heilbroner, "When Tomorrow Comes," *New York Times Book Review,* March 24, 1957, p. 6.
30. Peter F. Drucker, *America's Next Twenty Years* (New York: Harper & Brothers, 1957), p. 3.
31. Heilbroner, "When Tomorrow Comes."
32. Drucker, *Next Twenty Years,* p. 28.
33. Ibid., pp. 18–19.
34. Ibid., pp. 28–29.
35. Manuel Castells, *The Rise of the Network Society* (Oxford: Blackwell, 1996), pp. 257, 273, 272. (The indented quotations are from Castells, spliced from two separate pages; the quotation in the body of the paragraph is from a scholarly paper cited by Castells.)
36. Heilbroner, "When Tomorrow Comes."

37. Drucker, *Next Twenty Years*, p. 113.

38. Ibid., p. 12; for Thurow comment, see "Like Oil and Water: A Tale of Two Economists" by Louis Uchitelle in the Business Section of the *New York Times*, February 16, 1997, p. 1; for wages and productivity, see Sweeny, *America Needs a Raise*, p. 37.

39. Drucker, *Next Twenty Years*, p. 62.

40. Ibid., pp. 102–103.

41. Peter F. Drucker, "The Age of Social Transformation," in the *Atlantic Monthly* (November, 1994), p. 55.

42. E. J. Dionne, *They Only Look Dead* (New York: Simon & Schuster, 1996), p. 312.

43. Drucker, *Landmarks*, p. xvi.

44. Ibid.

45. Drucker, *New Society*, pp. 328, 331; for "Communism," see p. 248; for "militarization," see p. 222; for "The first step," see p. 262.

46. Drucker, *Landmarks*, pp. xv, xvi.

47. Ibid., pp. 4, 5.

48. Ibid., pp. 22–23.

49. Ibid., pp. 68, 105.

50. Ibid., p. 115.

51. Ibid., p. 121.

52. Drucker, *Landmarks*, p. 265.

53. Drucker, *The Ecological Vision*, p. 425.

54. Ibid., p. 434.

55. Ibid., p. 437.

*Chapter 6: Inventing Management*

1. Drucker interview with Warren Bennis, "The Invention of Management," in *Directors & Boards*, Winter 1982, p. 17.

2. For "Root," see Drucker, *The Ecological Vision*, p. 153; Alfred D. Chandler, Jr., *The Visible Hand* (Cambridge: Harvard University Press, 1977), p. 43.

3. Ibid., p. 204.

4. Drucker, *Practice*, p. ix.

5. Ibid., p. xi.

6. Alexander R. Heron, "Institutional Bosses," in *Saturday Review*, 38, January 22, 1955, p. 56; *Business Week*, "Study of a Costly Resource," December 18, 1954, p. 70; Drucker, *Frontiers*, p. 9.

7. Drucker, *Practice*, p. 3.

8. Ibid., pp. 3, 4, 12, 34.

9. Ibid., pp. 146, 341, 349.

10. Alan M. Kantrow, "Why Read Peter Drucker?," *Harvard Business Review,* January–February 1980, p. 81; for "dark forces," see Drucker, *The Age of Discontinuity*, p. xxiv.

11. Drucker, *Practice,* p. 6.

12. Ibid., p. 7.

13. Ibid., p. 12.

14. Ibid., p. 37; for "moving part," see "Drucker and the Art of Studied Simplicity," *Financial Times* (London), p. 12.

15. Drucker, *Practice,* p. 382.

16. Ibid., p. 383; Drucker, *The Ecological Vision*, p. 389; Drucker, *Management: Tasks, Responsibilities, Practices*, p. 40.

17. Drucker, *Practice,* p. 392.

18. *American Banker,* December 28, 1979; Drucker, *Practice,* pp. 49, 50.

19. Drucker, *Practice,* p. 49.

20. Ibid., pp. 50, 115.

21. Ibid., p. 51.

22. Author interview with Drucker, December 1995.

23. Drucker, *Practice,* pp. 114, 116-17.

24. For "commonplaces," see "Management Theorists: Peter Drucker, Salvationist," in *The Economist,* October 1, 1994, p. 83; Drucker, *Practice,* p. 114; for "Tarrant," see Tarrant, p. 77; Drucker, *Management,* p. 384; Drucker, *Practice,* p. 141.

25. For "Deming," see Andrea Gabor, *The Man Who Discovered Quality* (New York: Random House, 1990), pp. 21–22; Tarrant, pp. 157, 147.

26. Drucker, *Practice,* p. 144.

27. Ibid., p. 261.

28. Ibid., p. 264.

29. Ibid., p. 265; Drucker, *The Effective Executive*, p. 174; Drucker, *Management,* p. 421.

30. Drucker, *Practice,* p. 269.

31. Ibid., p. 272.

32. Ibid., pp. 278, 279; Bell, *The End of Ideology*, p. 251.

33. Ibid., p. 232.

34. Drucker, *Practice,* p. 281; Drucker, *Post-Capitalist Society*, pp. 33, 35, 292; Drucker, *Practice,* p. 284.

35. Drucker, *Practice,* p. 293.

36. Ibid., p. 293.

37. Drucker, *Management,* p. 269; Abraham H. Maslow, *Eupsychian Management* (Homewood, IL: Richard D. Irwin Inc. and the Dorsey Press, 1965), p. 27.

38. Richard H. Pells, *The Liberal Mind in a Conservative Age* (New York: Harper & Row), p. 187; William H. Whyte, *The Organization Man* (New York: Simon & Schuster, 1956), p. 235.

39. Drucker, *Effective Executive,* p. 75; Drucker, *Management,* p. 433.

40. Emile Durkheim, "On Anomie," in *Images of Man* (New York: Braziller, 1960), p. 477; Drucker, *Practice,* p. 267.

41. Drucker, *Managing for Results* (New York: HarperCollins, 1993), p. vii.

42. Ibid., pp. 5, 6, 7.

43. Ibid., pp. 63, 66; author's interview with Glen Urban, Dean of the Sloan School of Management, MIT; David J. Collis and Cynthia A. Montgomery, *Corporate Strategy* (Chicago: Irwin, 1997), p. 17.

44. Drucker, *Effective Executive,* p. 44.

45. Ibid., p. 1.

46. Ibid., pp. 23–24.

47. Drucker, *Effective Executive,* pp. 9, 25.

48. Ibid., p. 52.

49. Ibid., pp. 24, 75.

50. Ibid., pp. 24, 108, 109.

51. For "jazz," see interview with Drucker in *Wired,* August 1996, p. 119; Drucker, *Effective Executive,* pp. 52, 159; for interview in next paragraph, see Drucker, *Great Change,* p. 351; for Sloan, see profile of Drucker in *Forbes,* March 10, 1997, p. 125.

52. Drucker, *Management,* pp. 15, 419.

53. Ibid., pp. 12, 13.

54. Ibid., p. 16.

55. Ibid., pp. 9, 10, 13.

56. Ibid., p. 28.

57. Ibid., p. 176; Drucker, *The New Realities,* p. 188; for "blue collar," see Dudley Buffa and Michael Hais, "How Knowledge Workers Vote," in *Fast Company,* October-November 1996, p. 70.

58. For male wages since 1979, see Richard D. Freeman, "Toward an Apartheid Economy?" *Harvard Business Review,* September-October 1996, p. 116.

59. For "soap," see Drucker, *Effective Executive,* p. 4; Drucker, *Management,* p. 33.

60. Drucker, *Management,* pp. 407, 408, 409.

61. Ibid., pp. 809, 810.

*Chapter 7. The Age of Discontinuity*

1. Drucker, *The Age of Discontinuity,* p. xi.

2. Ibid., p. xxvii.

3. Ibid., pp. 4, 10.

4. Ibid., pp. 7, 2, 24.

5. Ibid., p. 29.

6. Ibid., p. xxvi.

7. Ibid., p. 36. Drucker, *Managing for the Future,* p. 19; the "Dallas" story I owe to Dudley Hafner, former CEO of the American Heart Association.

8. Drucker, *The Age of Discontinuity,* p. 38.

9. In Jeremy Rifkin, *The End of Work* (New York: Putnam, 1995), p. 103; for "$50,000 a day," see Joseph B. White "Re-Engineering Gurus Take Steps to Remodel Their Stalling Vehicles," in the *Wall Street Journal,* p. 1, November 26, 1996.

10. Drucker, *The Age of Discontinuity,* pp. 291, 292, 293, 295, 296.

11. Mary Harrington Hall, "A Conversation with Peter F. Drucker," in *Psychology Today,* May, 1968, p. 71; Drucker, *The Age of Discontinuity,* p. 296.

12. Rifkin, *End of Work,* p. 223.

13. David Riesman, *Individualism Reconsidered* (New York: The Free Press, 1964), p. 312; Bell, *The End of Ideology,* p. 258.

14. Drucker, *Frontiers,* p. 5.

15. Drucker, *The Age of Discontinuity,* pp. 81, 156.

16. Ibid., p. 158.

17. Ibid., p. 81.

18. Ibid., p. 101.

19. Ibid., p. 213.

20. Ibid., p. 215.

21. Ibid., p. 225.

22. Ibid., pp. 226, 229, 230.

23. Ibid., p. 233; for GI Bill, see Michael J. Bennett, *When Dreams Came Through* (Washington, D.C.: Brassey's, 1996).

24. Drucker, *The Age of Discontinuity,* p. 236.

25. Ibid., p. 241.

26. Ibid., p. 225.

27. Ibid., p. 321; for Bok, see *The State of the Nation,* p. 425; for "growth industry," see interview in Drucker, *Great Change,* p. 343.

28. Drucker, *The Age of Discontinuity,* p. 332.

29. Drucker, *Managing for the Future,* p. 11.

30. Drucker, *The New Realities,* pp. 19–23.

31. Peter F. Drucker, *The Pension Fund Revolution* (New Brunswick, NJ: Transaction Publishers, 1996), p. 6.

32. Drucker, *The Ecological Vision,* p. 265.

33. Drucker, *Frontiers,* p. 209.

34. Ibid., p. 215.

35. Drucker, *Pension Fund,* p. 3.

36. Ibid., pp. 58, 71.

37. Ibid., pp. 164, 165.

38. Jason Epstein, "Capitalism and Socialism: Declining Returns," in *The New York Review of Books,* February 17, 1977, p. 36.

*Chapter 8: Bring Your Own Machete*

1. For this paragraph, see "The Hostile Takeover and Its Discontents," in Drucker, *The Ecological Vision,* pp. 249–71.

2. Drucker, *The Ecological Vision,* p. 251; for "recent estimate," see Collis and Montgomery, *Corporate Strategy,* p. 2.

3. Drucker, *The Ecological Vision,* p. 250.

4. Ibid., pp. 258, 259; Drucker, *The Pension Fund Revolution,* p. 213.

5. Drucker, *The Ecological Vision,* p. 260.

6. Drucker, *Post-Capitalist Society,* p. 80; Drucker, *The Ecological Vision,* p. 254.

7. *Industry Week,* April 18, 1988, p. 26.

8. Drucker, *The Ecological Vision,* p. 254.

9. Drucker, *Innovation,* p. vii.

10. Drucker, *Frontiers,* p. 9.

11. Drucker, *Innovation,* pp. 2, 3.

12. Ibid., p. 24.

13. Drucker, *Innovation,* p. 139; Drucker, *Drucker on Asia,* p. 109; for "manager," see Drucker, *Great Change,* p. 17.

14. Drucker, *The Ecological Vision,* p. 107.

15. Ibid., pp. 111–13.

16. Drucker, *The Ecological Vision,* p. 111.

17. Drucker, *Innovation,* pp. 1–13.

18. Castells, *The Rise of the Network Society,* p. 61.

19. *Wall Street Journal* citation is from an undated clip; for *New York Times* citation, see "Illness Is Turning Into Financial Catastrophe" by Peter T. Kilborn, August 1, 1997, p. A10. For "small firms," see Robert Z. Lawrence, "Is it the economy, stupid?" in *Why People Don't Trust Government* (Cambridge, MA: Harvard University Press, 1997), p. 118; Freeman, *Harvard Business Review, op. cit.,* pp. 119–26.

20. Drucker, *Economic Man,* p. 134.

21. Drucker, *Great Change,* p. 236.

22. Ibid., p. 252.

23. From an interview with Peter Drucker; for "changing the human being,"

from Drucker, *Great Change,* p. 256; Nicolaus Mills, *The Triumph of Meanness* (Boston: Houghton Mifflin, 1997), pp. 80–83.

24. Ibid., p. 257; Drucker, "What Business Can Learn from Nonprofits," in *Harvard Business Review,* July/August 1989, p. 1.

25. Drucker, *Great Change,* p. 228; see review of Blank's book by Theda Skocpol, "The Next Liberalism," in the *Atlantic Monthly,* April 1997, p. 119.

26. Drucker, *Managing the Non-Profit,* p. xiv; Drucker, *The New Realities,* p. 200.

27. Peter Baida, "Doing Good Well," *New York Times Book Review,* 10/28/90, p. 21.

28. Drucker, *Managing the Non-Profit,* pp. 58, 71, 120, 148, 193, 197, 277, 278.

29. Ibid., p. 19.

30. Drucker, *Post-Capitalist Society,* p. 45.

31. Ibid., pp. 3, 42, 44.

32. Drucker, *Great Change,* p. 236.

33. Ibid., pp. 351–52.

# Indexed List of Books
## by Peter Drucker